ClassNotes and Study Guide

to accompany
Computer Concepts

SHELLY AND CASHMAN TITLES FROM BOYD & FRASER

Computer Concepts
Computer Concepts with BASIC
    ClassNotes and Study Guide to Accompany Computer Concepts and Computer Concepts with BASIC
Computer Concepts with Microcomputer Applications (Lotus® version)
Computer Concepts with Microcomputer Applications (VP-Planner Plus® version)
    ClassNotes and Study Guide to Accompany Computer Concepts with Microcomputer Applications
    (VP-Planner Plus® and Lotus® versions)
Learning to Use WordPerfect® Lotus 1-2-3® and dBASE III PLUS®
    ClassNotes and Study Guide to Accompany Learning to Use WordPerfect® Lotus 1-2-3® and dBASE III PLUS®
Learning to Use WordPerfect® VP-Planner Plus® and dBASE III PLUS®
    ClassNotes and Study Guide to Accompany Learning to Use WordPerfect® VP-Planner Plus® and dBASE III PLUS®
Learning to Use WordPerfect®
    ClassNotes and Study Guide to Accompany Learning to Use WordPerfect®
Learning to Use VP-Planner Plus®
    ClassNotes and Study Guide to Accompany Learning to Use VP-Planner Plus®
Learning to Use Lotus 1-2-3®
    ClassNotes and Study Guide to Accompany Learning to Use Lotus 1-2-3®
Learning to Use dBASE III PLUS®
    ClassNotes and Study Guide to Accompany Learning to Use dBASE III PLUS®
Computer Fundamentals with Application Software
    Workbook and Study Guide to Accompany Computer Fundamentals with Application Software
Learning to Use SuperCalc®3 dBASE III® and WordStar® 3.3: An Introduction
Learning to Use SuperCalc®3: An Introduction
Learning to Use dBASE III®: An Introduction
Learning to Use WordStar® 3.3: An Introduction
BASIC Programming for the IBM Personal Computer
Turbo Pascal Programming

FORTHCOMING SHELLY AND CASHMAN TITLES

RPG II and III   Systems Analysis and Design

ClassNotes and Study Guide

to accompany
Computer Concepts

Shelly • Cashman • Waggoner

Boyd & Fraser

The Shelly & Cashman Series

Boyd & Fraser

ISBN 0-87835-369-0

Written, developed, and produced by HyperGraphics and Solomon & Douglas
Manufactured in the United States of America

HyperGraphics® is a registered trademark of HyperGraphics Corporation

10 9 8 7 6 5 4 3 2

CONTENTS

CHAPTER 1   AN INTRODUCTION TO COMPUTERS 1.1

CHAPTER 2   MICROCOMPUTER APPLICATIONS: USER TOOLS 2.1

CHAPTER 3   PROCESSING DATA INTO INFORMATION 3.1

CHAPTER 8 FILE ORGANIZATION AND DATABASES 8.1

CHAPTER 9 DATA COMMUNICATIONS 9.1

CHAPTER 10 OPERATING SYSTEMS AND SYSTEM SOFTWARE 10.1

CHAPTER 11 COMMERCIAL APPLICATION SOFTWARE 11.1

CHAPTER 12   THE INFORMATION SYSTEM DEVELOPMENT LIFE CYCLE   12.1

CHAPTER 13   PROGRAM DEVELOPMENT   13.1

CHAPTER 14   CAREER OPPORTUNITIES   14.1

CHAPTER 15   TRENDS AND ISSUES IN THE INFORMATION AGE   15.1

INTRODUCTION TO DOS   DOS 1

PREFACE TO THE STUDENT

The teaching and learning process has changed little over the past years, even with the advent of personal computers and technology. The *ClassNotes and Study Guide* supplement to your Shelly and Cashman textbook is designed to lead the way to the betterment of the teaching and learning process by allowing interaction and participation throughout the teaching and learning process. This supplement can be used in the classroom, in the laboratory, or as a stand-alone study guide.

IN THE CLASSROOM

If your instructor uses the HyperGraphics software in the classroom, you can follow the lecture and take notes by using this supplement. As topics are presented by your instructor, you can fill in the blanks and label the diagrams. Your notetaking chores will be greatly reduced, and your chances of mastering the course materials will increase.

IN THE LABORATORY

The HyperGraphics software that accompanies your Shelly and Cashman text can be made available to you in your computer laboratory, if your instructor chooses to do so. In that case you can use the *ClassNotes and Study Guide* in the computer lab. As you review the materials using HyperGraphics, you can actively work in this supplement to capture the essentials of each chapter.

AS A STAND-ALONE STUDY GUIDE

ClassNotes and Study Guide can also be used as a stand-alone study guide. Each chapter reviews key concepts of each textbook chapter using diagrams, illustrations, and questions.

ACKNOWLEDGEMENTS

We wish to thank Tom Walker, Vice President and Publisher at Boyd & Fraser, for his vision and belief in the innovative HyperGraphics classroom delivery system. His commitment to excellence and quality is clearly illustrated in the resulting system. We thank Mary Douglas, director of production, for her guidance and patience as we endeavored to produce an innovative study guide that would benefit both student and instructor. A special thanks to Susan Solomon, director of development, whose contributions resulted in the synergy between HyperGraphics and the ClassNotes product. Her influence in the methodology and approaches are contained in all aspects of both the software and print materials. Finally, thanks to the HyperGraphics staff, who created the software to accompany the textbook and the ClassNotes. They have produced the first complete classroom delivery system for a major textbook, and their efforts will be apparent as students and instructors alike use the HyperGraphics software.

Chapter 1

An Introduction to Computers

Objectives

1. Explain what a computer is and how it processes data to produce information.
2. Identify the four operations of the information processing cycle: input, process, output, and storage.
3. Explain how the operations of the information processing cycle are performed by computer hardware and software.
4. Identify the major categories of computers.
5. Describe the six elements of an information system: equipment, software, data, personnel, users, and procedures.
6. Discuss how computers are used in the modern world.
7. Describe the evolution of the computer industry.

Chapter Outline

WHAT IS A COMPUTER?

1. A computer is a collection of devices that function together to process _output_ .

WHAT DOES A COMPUTER DO?

1. List the four general operations that all computers perform.

input   _process_

output   _storage_

2. The four general operations listed above together can be called the _information processing cycle_

3. List examples of data.   4. List examples of information.

words   _letters_

numbers   _forecasts_

pictures   _presentations_

5. _information processing_ or _electronic data processing_ is the process of converting data into

information.

6. Information and data are retained on _output_ devices.

7-10. Label the following diagram, choosing from the following list.

input	storage
processor	main memory
output	user
	printer

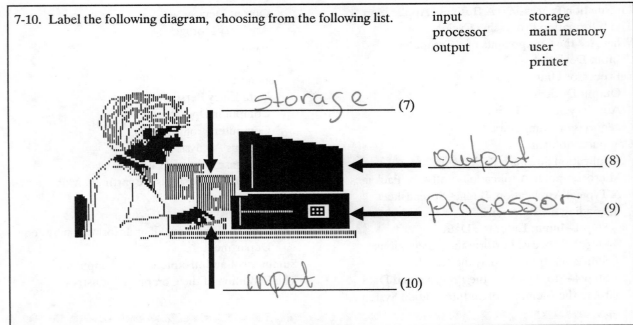

storage (7)

output (8)

processor (9)

input (10)

WHY IS A COMPUTER SO POWERFUL?

1. The power of a computer is derived from its ability to perform four primary operations. List these operations in their correct order by choosing from the list below.

logic   input   *input*

storage   process   *process*

arithmetic   output   *output*

                                          storage

2. A computer is powerful because of the way it executes the information processing cycle. What three words best describe how the computer executes this cycle?

_____

_____

_____

HOW DOES A COMPUTER KNOW WHAT TO DO?

1. A computer follows a detailed set of *instuctions* .

2. These instructions can also be called *Computer* *program* or *program instructions software*

INFORMATION PROCESSING: A BUSINESS APPLICATION

1-2. Label the following diagram.

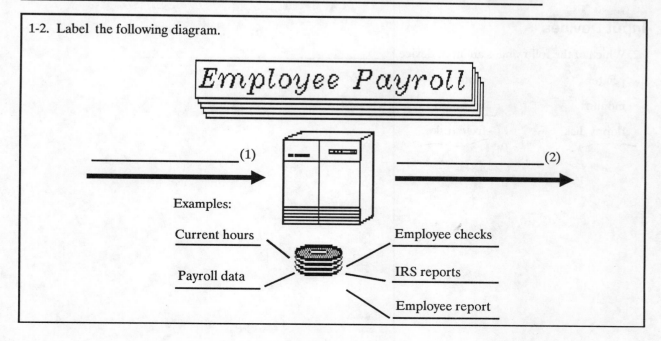

Employee Payroll

(1)

(2)

Examples:

Current hours

Payroll data

Employee checks

IRS reports

Employee report

THE INFORMATION PROCESSING CYCLE

1-4. Label the information processing cycle.

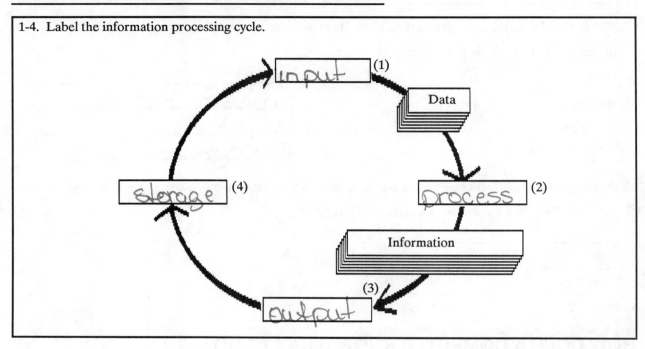

WHAT ARE THE COMPONENTS OF A COMPUTER?

1. List the computer hardware components.

_____   _____

_____   _____

Input Devices

2. Which of the following is an input device? _____

printer   plotter

monitor   keyboard

floppy disk   fixed disk

Processor Unit

3. List the arithmetic operations a computer performs. Choose your answers from this list.

addition   sine/cosine   _____

square root   subtraction   _____

multiplication   division   _____

                                     _____

4. List the logical operations that compare data.

_____

_____

_____

5. Main memory or primary storage electronically stores _____ and

_____ currently being used.

6. The processor unit is also referred to as the _____

or _____ .

Output Devices

7. Give some examples of output devices from the following list.

computer screen   printer   hard disk   _____

scanner   keyboard   diskette   _____

Auxiliary Storage Units

8. Auxiliary storage stores _____ and _____ not

currently being used.

9. All components of the computer except the processor unit are called _____ .

CATEGORIES OF COMPUTERS

1. From the list below, identify the four categories of computers.

   maxicomputer   supercomputer   _____

   minicomputer   maxiframe computer   _____

   hypercomputer   mainframe computer   _____

   hybridcomputer   microcomputer   _____

2. From the list below, identify the characteristics common to all computers.

   monitor   speed   _____

   size   processing capabilities _____

   price   keyboard   _____

   floppy disk   _____

3. Computers can be categorized by their price. Fill in the appropriate price ranges below.

   Microcomputers: _____   Mainframe computers: _____

   Minicomputers: _____   Supercomputers: _____

COMPUTER SOFTWARE

1. What are the four commonly used types of application software packages?

   _____   _____

   _____   _____

In questions 2 through 6, complete the steps that a user takes when using an application software package.

Choose from the list below.

   retrieve   load   process   output

   save   data   information

2. _____ the application program.

3. Provide _____ to the application program.

4. Utilize the application program to _____ the data.

5. _____ the information to a printer.

6. _____ the information on disk.

WHAT ARE THE ELEMENTS OF AN INFORMATION SYSTEM?

1. List the six elements of an information system.

_____   _____

_____   _____

_____   _____

A TOUR OF AN INFORMATION SYSTEMS DEPARTMENT

1. A _____ provides multiple users with computing resources.

2. Multiuser computers are managed by departments within an organization. Typically, the departments will be called the _____ , _____ , or _____ department.

Equipment

Input Devices

3. List at least two input devices.

_____   _____

Processor

4. The _____ performs the major processing of data and information.

Output Devices

5. List at least two output devices.

_____   _____

Auxiliary Storage

6. List at least two auxiliary storage devices.

_____   _____

7. Magnetic disk devices are both _____ and _____ .

8. A _____ holds information in an organized fashion for future reference.

Software

9. Software is generally maintained on what two types of storage media? _____

   or _____ .

10. Software is placed into _____ when it is required by a user.

Data

11. Data is obtained from _____ entered directly by users and personnel.

Personnel

12. List the six types of personnel in an information systems department.

   _____   _____

   _____   _____

   _____   _____

13-16. Fill in the organization chart for an IS department.

```
                    ┌──────────────────────────┐
                    │                      (13) │
                    │                           │
                    └─────────────┬─────────────┘
           ┌──────────────────────┼──────────────────────┐
    ┌───────────────┐    ┌───────────────┐    ┌───────────────┐
    │         (14)  │    │         (15)  │    │         (16)  │
    │               │    │               │    │               │
    └───────────────┘    └───────────────┘    └───────────────┘
```

Users

17. List three activities of users.

   _____

   _____

   _____

Procedures

18. _____ are typically written in manuals and technical documents.

THE EVOLUTION OF THE COMPUTER INDUSTRY

1-17.   Fill in as many key events below as possible without consulting your book.

Dr. Kemeny: BASIC	IBM 360	IBM: Software unbundled
FORTRAN	IBM	Dr. Hoff: Microprocessor
DEC Minicomputer	Jobs & Wozniak: Apple	Microsoft: MS-DOS
Transistors	Dr. Hopper	IBM: Application System 400
UNIVAC I	VisiCalc	Kapor: Lotus 1-2-3
IBM PC	Intel 80386	

1952 _____ (1)

_____ (2)

_____ (3)

1957 _____ (4)

1958 _____ (5)

1964 _____ (6)

1965 _____ (7)

_____ (8)

1969 _____ (9)

_____ (10)

1976 _____ (11)

1979 _____ (12)

1980 _____ (13)

1981 _____ (14)

1983 _____ (15)

1987 _____ (16)

1988 _____ (17)

REVIEW

1. A computer is a collection of devices that function together to process _____ .
   a. numbers   c. data
   b. words   d. information

2. The information processing cycle is comprised of input, processing, output,
   and _____ .

3. _____ is created from data during the processing phase of the information processing cycle.

    a. Information

    b. Output

    c. Input

    d. A computer program

    e. Storage

4. T   F   The production of information by processing data on a computer is called information processing or electronic data processing.

5. T   F   One reason a computer is powerful is due to its storage capability.

6. T   F   Because computer operations occur at exceptionally fast speeds, the electronic circuits fail on a frequent basis.

7. Instructions that direct the operations of a computer are called _____ .

8. Several different forms of _____ can be produced from a single set of data.

    a. input

    b. programs

    c. processing

    d. storage

    e. information

9. T   F   The information processing cycle is fundamental to understanding computers and how they process data into information.

10. A keyboard is an example of an _____ .

11. All arithmetic and logical processing takes place in the _____ .

    a. main memory

    b. controller

    c. processor

    d. program

    e. none of the above

12. Which of the following is part of the CPU?

    a. auxiliary memory

    b. main memory

    c. secondary memory

    d. the input unit

    e. a peripheral device

13. A printer is an example of what type of device?

    a. input device

    b. auxiliary storage device

    c. primary memory device

    d. output device

    e. none of the above

14. T   F   Auxiliary storage units are used to store instructions and data when they are not being used by the processor.

15. These computers are the fastest computers available.

    a. supercomputers   d. microcomputers

    b. mainframe computers   e. none of the above

    c. superminicomputers

16. **T   F**   At this point in time, minicomputers fall between microcomputers and mainframe computers in price and power.

17. These computers are also called personal computers.

    a. supercomputers   d. microcomputers

    b. mainframe computers   e. none of the above

    c. minicomputers

18. **T   F**   A computer program or software specifies the sequence of operations that are to be performed.

19. Purchased programs are often referred to as _____ packages.

20. How many elements comprise an information system?

    a. five   d. two

    b. six   e. eight

    c. three

21. _____ typically initiate requests to the information systems department.

    a. Database administrators   d. Computer operators

    b. Computer programmers   e. Users

    c. Systems analysts

22. The _____ has the responsibility for designing new application systems that will be computerized.

    a. database administrator   d. Vice President of Information Systems

    b. system manager   e. computer programmer

    c. systems analyst

23. The _____ has the responsibility of managing the totality of data within an organization.

    a. database administrator   d. Vice President of Information Systems

    b. system manager   e. computer programmer

    c. systems analyst

Chapter 2

Microcomputer Applications: User Tools

Objectives

1. Identify the four most widely used general microcomputer software applications.
2. Describe how each of the four applications can help users.
3. Explain the key features of each of the four major microcomputer applications.
4. Describe the key features of data communications and desktop publishing software.
5. Explain integrated software and its advantages.
6. List and describe five guidelines for purchasing software application packages.
7. Discuss tips for using each of the four major microcomputer applications.

Chapter Outline

AN INTRODUCTION TO GENERAL MICROCOMPUTER APPLICATIONS

1. A _____ user knows how to use the computer to solve problems but doesn't necessarily know how to repair a computer.

2. For general microcomputer applications there will be a _____ range of users who are computer literate. Choose your answer from the following.   narrow   broad   small

3. Applications that are deemed "easy to use" are typically referred to as _____ .

4. List some features of a "good" user interface. Choose your answers from the following list.

   function keys   menus   interactivity   screen prompts   icons   response time

   _____   _____

   _____   _____

5-7. Label the diagram below. Choose your answers from the following list.

   function keys   menus   interactivity   screen prompts   icons   response time

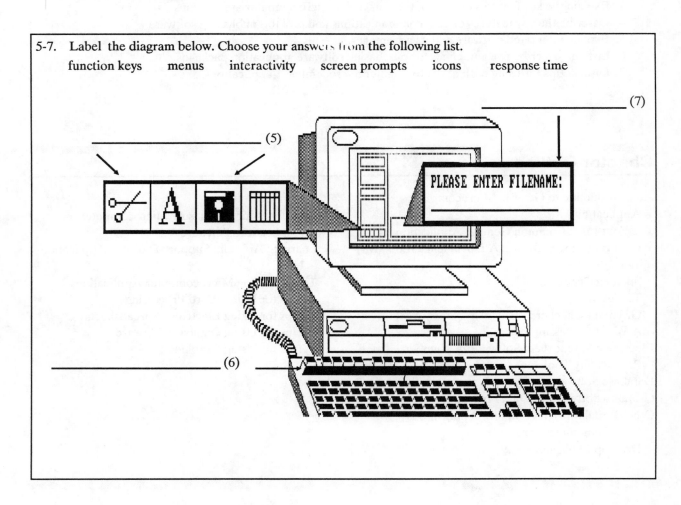

PLEASE ENTER FILENAME:

THE FOUR MOST COMMON GENERAL APPLICATIONS

1. List the four most common general microcomputer applications.

   Choose your applications from the following.

   word processing   CAD/CAM   electronic spreadsheet   graphics

   database   desktop publishing   scientific computing

   _____   _____

   _____   _____

WORD PROCESSING SOFTWARE: A DOCUMENT PRODUCTIVITY TOOL

1. Which of the following are advantages of word processing software over typewriting?

   Choose your answers from the following list.

   online spell checking   merge/retyping capability   _____

   faster   online thesaurus   _____

   more accurate   hardware reliability   _____

   less tedious   _____

2. Which of the items in the list in Question 1 above allow the user to correct misspelled words?

   _____

   _____

   _____

3. Basic editing functions allow users to _____ , _____ ,

   and _____ characters.

4. Duplicating blocks of text is often called the _____ function.

5. To reorder blocks of text, a user uses the _____ function.

6. Altering the appearances of characters can provide text emphasis. Which of the following are ways in which characters can be altered?

boldfacing   underlining   _____

blinking   changing fonts   _____

using graphics   _____

7. The user may indent text or create multiple columns of text in a document. Choosing such operations to change the appearance of a document is referred to as _____ the text.

8. _____ perform automatic operations to identify and correct spelling errors.

9. _____ can be used to provide synonyms for identified words within a document and then to substitute that synonym within the text.

10. _____ will detect and correct grammar mistakes and incorrect sentence structure.

11. A user can specify a variety of options when printing a document. Which of the following are some of the options?

change margins   vary printing speed   _____

change paper type   change print style   _____

change page size   _____

Complete 12-14 below. The flexibility of document handling and processing includes:

12. the ability to _____ a document, even though it has already been printed once

13. the ability to _____ a document electronically and to recall quickly and use the document

14. _____ a document over phone lines to a another location

The operations that a word processor performs can be categorized into four main features. In 15-18, write the feature for each list of common items.

15. The following items are examples of the _____ feature.

insert character   move paragraph

insert word   move blocks

insert line   merge text

move sentence

16. The following items are examples of the _____ feature.

    delete character   delete paragraph

    delete word   delete document

    delete sentence

17. The following items are examples of the _____ feature.

    scroll line up/down   enhance character

    scroll page up/down   format display

    word wrap

18. The following items are examples of the _____ feature.

    set page format   select spacing

    select fonts   auto-paginate

    enhance characters   print page range

    adjust print size

ELECTRONIC SPREADSHEET SOFTWARE: A NUMBER PRODUCTIVITY TOOL

1. List four advantages of spreadsheet software over the calculator/pencil.

_____   _____

_____   _____

2. _____ , _____ , and _____

    are the major organizational components of the electronic spreadsheet.

3-5. Label the following diagrams. Choose your answers from the following.

row   spreadsheet   column   bar   cell   line

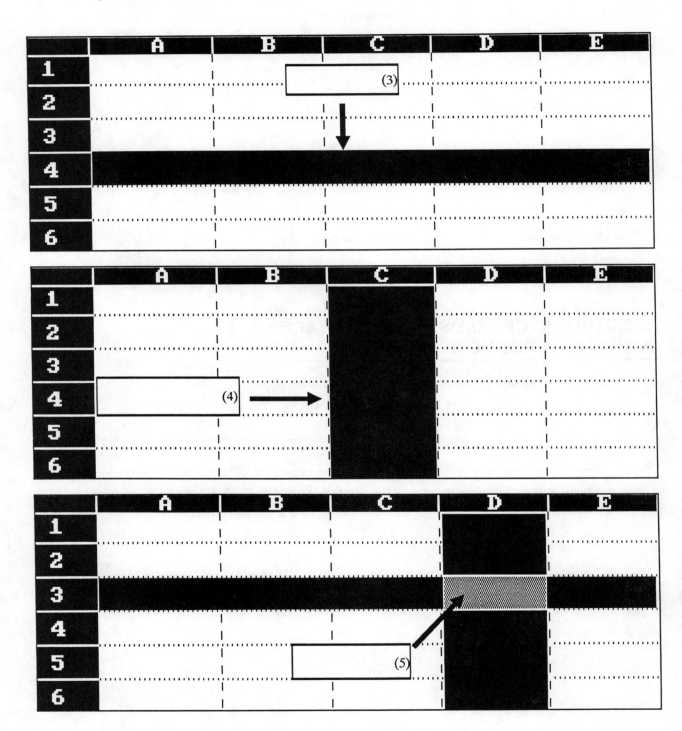

6. List the three cell types. Choose your answers from the following.

macros   labels

formulas   functions

values

_____

_____

_____

7. The process of _____ occurs when a value is changed and all other values that are affected by this change are updated automatically.

8. _____ analysis is possible by speculating on changes for certain cells or values, and then observing the effect of the changes on the total spreadsheet. For example, one could change the selling price of a particular product and observe the effect of regional and national sales dollars forecasts.

The operations that spreadsheet software performs can be categorized into six main features. For 9-14, write the feature for each list of common items.

9. The following items are examples of the _____ feature.

global format   delete column

insert column   delete row

insert row   set up titles

set up windows

10. The following items are examples of the _____ feature.

format data range   erase cells

11. The following items are examples of the _____ feature.

copy from cells   copy to cells

12. The following items are examples of the _____ feature.

move from cells   move to cells

13. The following items are examples of the _____ feature.

save   erase

retrieve   list

14. The following items are examples of the _____ feature.

set up margins   define print range

define header   define page length

define footer

DATABASE SOFTWARE: A DATA MANAGEMENT TOOL

1. List the three major functions of data management software. Choose your answers from the following.

   manipulate data   convert data   _____

   update data   retrieve data   _____

   file data   _____

2. The concept of a _____ is equivalent to a manila folder containing data.

3. A _____ is analogous to a form within the manila folder.

4. A _____ is comparable to an individual piece of data within the form.

5. A _____ compared to file management pertains to multiple related files within a

   business entity.

The operations that database software performs can be categorized into four main features. For 6-9, write the

feature for each list of common items.

6. The following items are examples of the _____ feature.

   clear all   create   join

   close   delete   recall

   copy   erase   rename

   select   sort   total

   use

7. The following items are examples of the _____ feature.

   browse   list

   display   report

8. The following items are examples of the _____ feature.

   browse   edit

   change   replace

   update

9. The following items are examples of the _____ feature.

   average   count and sum

GRAPHICS SOFTWARE: A DATA PRESENTATION TOOL

1-3. Label the three common forms of data representation in graphic forms. Choose your answers from the

following.   pie chart   bar chart   spline graph   line graph

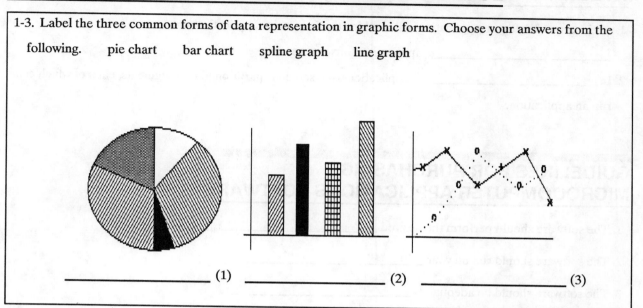

_____ (1)   _____ (2)   _____ (3)

4. The use of graphics to deliver concepts and ideas in a group format is called _____

graphics.

5. Graphics are termed _____ when numbers input by users are transformed into

graphics.

6. Graphics are termed _____ when the user issues commands to create the specific

graphics.

OTHER POPULAR MICROCOMPUTER APPLICATIONS

Data Communications

1. In a _____ application, data is transferred between computers at remote

locations. Many times this form of data transfer occurs over normal telephone lines.

Desktop Publishing

2. In _____ applications, the user combines graphics and text to produce

documents in publication quality format.

INTEGRATED SOFTWARE

1. An integrated software application will combine the four major applications into

   _____ application software system.

2. In _____ applications, the screen is partitioned into segments, each of which can

   run an application.

GUIDELINES FOR PURCHASING
MICROCOMPUTER APPLICATIONS SOFTWARE

1. The software should perform the desired _____ .

2. The software should run on your _____ .

3. The software should be adequately _____ .

4. You should _____ the software from a reputable source.

5. You should attempt to obtain the best _____ .

LEARNING AIDS AND SUPPORT TOOLS FOR APPLICATION USERS

1. A _____ is a computer-based system for teaching the user the basic operations of

   the application.

2. _____ provides the user with immediate assistance while the user is utilizing the

   application software.

3. _____ provide printed documentation on the various applications.

4. _____ assist the user by providing visual assistance on which keys and key

   sequences are required for each function.

TIPS FOR USING MICROCOMPUTER APPLICATIONS

Tips for Using Word Processing

1. Learn how to move the _____ .

2. Consider how a _____ looks.

3. Use a _____ checker.

4. File your documents under _____ names.

5. Create document _____ .

6. _____ your work on a frequent basis.

Tips for Using Electronic Spreadsheets

7. State _____ clearly.

8. Use range names for key _____ .

9. Use meaningful row/column _____ .

10. Leave room for _____ .

11. _____ results.

12. _____ the spreadsheet in the spreadsheet.

Tips for Using Database Software

13. Take time to _____ the file first.

14. Use _____ file and field names.

15. Avoid using significant _____ numbers.

16. Let the system generate _____ .

17. Create an _____ file for frequent, non-ID access to another file.

Tips for Using Graphics

18. Take time to _____ each graphic.

19. Don't present too much _____ .

20. Choose the appropriate type of _____ .

21. Use _____ sparingly.

22. Use _____ carefully.

23. Be _____ .

24. Make _____ graphics simple.

REVIEW

1. T   F   "Computer literate" is a term used to describe individuals who know how to operate and program computers.

2. T   F   Icons refers to pictures displayed on the screen that are associated with various program options.

3. The four most popular microcomputer applications are word processing, database, spreadsheet, and _____ .

4. Word processing software is primarily involved with which of the following application areas?
    a. numeric manipulation   d. visual display development
    b. data organization/storage   e. forecasting
    c. document preparation

5. T   F   Thesaurus software allows the user to look up synonyms for words appearing in a word processing document.

6. Which of the following packages provides writing style analysis for word processing documents?
    a. spelling checker   d. format command
    b. thesaurus   e. grammar checker
    c. move command

7. Electronic spreadsheet software is primarily used to accomplish which one of the following tasks?
    a. organize fields, records, and   d. manage numeric data
       files   e. prepare a document
    b. develop graphics presentations
    c. spell check a document

8. Cells in an electronic spreadsheet may contain three types of data: labels, _____ , and numbers.

9. The ability of an electronic spreadsheet to recalculate when data is changed enables _____ testing.

10. A primary way in which database software differs from file management software is that database software works on _____ files together.

11. A _____ is a collection of related data items stored in a computer file.

12. _____ graphics is widely used by management personnel when reviewing and communicating information.

13. _____ software allows data stored on one computer to be transmitted to another computer.

14. Many people consider _____ to be similar to a desktop where the desk has multiple papers lying on it.

15. Even the best software may be unusable if the _____ does not clearly and completely describe the software.

16. _____ refers to additional instructions that are available on the screen without leaving the application.

Chapter 3

Processing Data Into Information

Objectives

1. Explain the four operations of the information processing cycle: input, process, output, and storage.
2. Define data and explain the terms used to organize data in an information processing system: field, record, file, database.
3. Discuss data management and explain why it is needed.
4. Explain arithmetic and logical processing.
5. Describe interactive processing and batch processing.
6. List and explain the qualities of information.

Chapter Outline

OVERVIEW OF THE INFORMATION PROCESSING CYCLE

1-4. In the diagram below, fill in the four components of the information processing cycle.

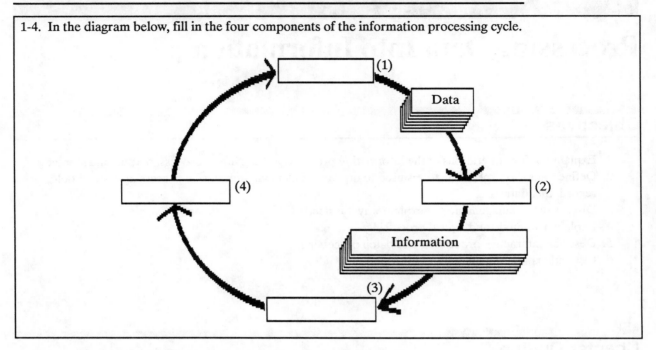

5-7. Give example(s) of the following information processing cycle components.

Choose your answers from the following.

fixed disk   floppy disk   keyboard   printer   computer screen

Input: _____ (5)

Output: _____ (6)

Auxiliary storage: _____ (7)

8. In the information processing cycle, _____ and _____

move from the input device into main memory. Draw arrows in the diagram below to show this movement.

9. _____ manages the input, processing, output, and auxiliary storage processes and resources during the information processing cycle.

10. In this process data is transformed into _____ .

WHAT IS DATA AND HOW IS IT ORGANIZED?

1. The three types of character data are:

   _____

   _____

   _____

2. The three types of fields are:

   _____

   _____

   _____

3. A _____ is an individual data item.

   A _____ is a collection of related fields.

   A _____ is a collection of related records.

4-6. In the diagram below circle a field, place a check mark next to a record, and draw a box around a file.

```
1250 Smith   Clerk     2540 01-Dec-87 1,250.00   500.00
1050 Wang    Salesman  2300 15-Apr-85 3,600.00
2300 Juarez  Manager   3510 01-Jan-80 4,200.00 1,500.00
1520 Adami   Salesman  2300 15-Jul-83 2,500.00   250.00
0010 Benito  President 0000 01-Aug-65 6,500.00
```

---

7. A _____ is an identified access path to a file and can be used to arrange the contents of a file into a specific order.

8. A collection of related files is called a _____ .

DATA MANAGEMENT

Fill in the blanks in the following statement. Choose your answers from the following.

methods   manuals   techniques   security   programs   procedures   maintenance

1. Data management refers to _____ , _____ ,

   and _____ that are used to manage data attributes and provide for

   the _____ and _____ of data.

Fill in the following statement about data management. Choose your answer from the following.

data outputs   data sources   processing

2. In an airline database, customers, schedulers, and inventory are examples

   of _____ .

3. List the major components of data attributes. Choose your answers from the following.

   reliable   available   consumable   accurate   timely   optimized

   _____   _____

   _____   _____

4. List the major components of data security. Choose your answers from the following.

   backup   authorized access   visible   available   timely

   _____   _____

5. List the major components of data maintenance. Choose your answers from the following.

   filing   adding   updating   changing   deleting   maintaining

   _____   _____

   _____   _____

6. List the major components of data integrity. Choose your answers from the following.

   data security   data timeliness   data reliability   data accuracy   data encoding

   _____

   _____

   _____

HOW THE INFORMATION PROCESSING CYCLE WORKS

For each component of the information processing cycle below, some key concept statements are given. Choose the correct answer for each key concept statement. Choose your answers from the list preceding each group of statements.

Input Operations

Choose your answers from the following.

main memory   keyboard   auxiliary storage   computer program   processing

1. Input operations involve the flow of data from input devices to _____ .

2. The _____ controls the operations of input, process, and output.

3. Data is always entered into main memory for _____ .

Processing Operations

Choose the best answers for 4 through 8 from the following.

path   output   input   arithmetic operations   multiple   repeated   recalculated   record   field

Arithmetic Operations

4. Programs can perform _____ on data in memory.

5. Answers from arithmetic operations can be used in other operations and as _____ .

6. Computers process one _____ at a time.

7. Program instructions may be _____ .

Logical Operations

8. Program instructions may compare data and then select an appropriate _____ to take based on the comparison results.

Output Operations

Choose your answers from the following.   results   information   data

9. Input produces _____ .

10. Processing produces _____ .

11. Output puts _____ in a usable form.

Storage Operations

Choose your answer from the following.   main memory   auxiliary storage

12. The transfer of programs, data, and information to _____ occurs during storage operations.

METHODS OF PROCESSING DATA INTO INFORMATION

Fill in the type of processing below. Choose your answers from the following.

interactive   transaction   batch   authorized   backup

1. In _____ processing, data is processed upon entry, and output is produced immediately.

2. In _____ processing, data is collected, and at some later time all the data is processed as a group.

3. In _____ processing, the user enters all of the data pertaining to a complete transaction prior to the processing of that data.

Fill in the blanks in the statement below about batch processing. Choose your answers from the following.

numeric   small   periodic   large

4. In batch processing applications, the application requires _____ processing of a _____ number of records.

5. List two examples of business activities that would be appropriate for batch processing.

_____   _____

QUALITIES OF INFORMATION

1. Complete the following list of qualities of information.

accurate   _____

verifiable   _____

timely   _____

organized

REVIEW

1. Which of the following is part of the information processing cycle?

    a. equipment   d. telecommunication

    b. input   e. personnel

    c. procedures

2. The information processing cycle is comprised of input, processing, output, and _____ .

    a. computing   d. arithmetic operations

    b. information   e. data

    c. storage

3. The operations in the information processing cycle are carried out by computer hardware and _____ .

    a. peripherals   c. software

    b. storage   d. logic

4. Input devices are used to enter both data and computer _____ into main memory.

    a. numbers   c. information

    b. systems   d. programs

5. T   F   Both the program and data must be in the main memory of the computer for processing to occur.

6. Secondary storage devices are also called _____ storage devices.

    a. binary   c. primary

    b. tertiary   d. auxiliary

7. Data is comprised of _____ .

    a. files   c. programs

    b. characters   d. information

8. Each fact or unique piece of data is referred to as a _____ .

    a. field   c. file

    b. word   d. record

9. The field "01/31/90" is called a(n) _____ field.

    a. numeric   c. alphanumeric

    b. character   d. data

10. A _____ is a collection of related fields.

    a. file   c. relational field

    b. program   d. record

11. A collection of records is called a _____ .

    a. database   c. field

    b. file   d. bit

12. The _____ field is used to arrange records in a specific order.

    a. key   c. last

    b. first   d. organization

13. In a _____ file organization records are not arranged in any particular order.

    a. sequential   c. random

    b. normal   d. unfixed

14. A _____ implies that a relationship has been established among multiple files.

    a. field   c. record

    b. file   d. database

15. The purpose of data management is to ensure that data is in the _____ form and available for processing.

    a. numeric   c. database

    b. correct   d. file

16. Data accuracy, reliable data entry, and timeliness are the three primary attributes of data _____ .

    a. integrity   c. availability

    b. security   d. fluency

17. T   F   Data security refers to protecting data to keep it from changing into information.

18. Updating data by adding, changing, and/or deleting information is part of data _____ .

    a. integrity   c. maintenance

    b. alteration   d. security

19. Processing operations define how the data will be _____ into a usable form.

    a. input   c. manipulated

    b. output   d. programmed

20. Addition, subtraction, multiplication, and division are examples of _____ processing.

    a. arithmetic   c. data

    b. logical   d. character

21. The ability to _____ instructions allows the processing of any number of records with one set of instructions.

    a. omit   c. move

    b. copy   d. repeat

22. Logical operations are the computer's ability to _____ data stored in main memory.

    a. relate   c. compare

    b. add   d. move

23. _____ are a common form of output that are often used by business people.

    a. Programs   c. Databases

    b. Reports   d. Cards

24. _____ operations refer to the transfer of programs, data, and information to auxiliary storage.

    a. Arithmetic   c. Storage

    b. Processing   d. Logical

25. _____ processing means that data is processed upon entry and output is produced immediately.

    a. Interactive   c. Information

    b. Batch   d. Data

26. In _____ processing, data is collected, and at some later time it is processed as a group.

    a. interactive   c. collective

    b. group   d. batch

27. In _____ processing, the computer user enters all the data pertaining to a complete transaction.

    a. interactive   c. transaction

    b. batch   d. data

28. Accurate, verifiable, timely, organized, meaningful, and cost effective are qualities of _____ .

    a. data   c. reports

    b. information   d. output

Chapter 4

Input to the Computer

Objectives

1. Define the four types of input and how the computer uses each type.
2. Describe the standard features of keyboards and explain how to use the cursor control and function keys.
3. Identify the two types of terminals and how to use each type.
4. Describe several input devices other than the keyboard and terminal.
5. Define user interface and explain how it has evolved.
6. Define the term menu and describe various forms of menus.
7. Discuss some of the features that should be included in a good user interface.
8. Discuss the differences between interactive and batch processing data entry.
9. Describe online and offline data entry and the uses for each.
10. List and explain the systems and procedures associated with data entry.
11. Explain the term ergonomics and describe some of the changes that have occurred in equipment design.

Chapter Outline

What Is Input?
The Keyboard
Terminals
  Dumb Terminals
  Intelligent Terminals
  Special Purpose Terminals
Other Input Devices
  The Mouse
  Touch Screens
  Graphic Input Devices
  Voice Input
Input Devices Designed for Specific Purposes
  Magnetic Ink Character Recognition
  Scanners
    Optical Character Readers
    Optical Mark Readers
    Laser Scanners
    Page Scanners
    Image Processing
  Data Collection Devices
User Interfaces

Evolution of User Interface Software
  Prompts
  Menus
    Sequential Number
    Alphabetic Selection
    Cursor Positioning
    Reverse Video
    Icon Selection
  Submenus
  Menus: Advantages and Disadvantages
Graphics
Features of a User Interface
Data Entry for Interactive and Batch Processing
  Data Entry for Interactive Processing
  Data Entry for Batch Processing
  Summary of Interactive and Batch Data Entry
An Example of Online Data Entry
  Order Entry Menu
  Enter Orders
Data Entry Procedures
Ergonomics
Summary of Input to the Computer

WHAT IS INPUT?

1. List the four major categories of input. Choose your answers from the following.

   information   programs   user responses   commands   data   documents

   _____   _____

   _____   _____

Fill in the blanks in questions 2-7 . Choose your answers from the following.

Note that some answers may be used more than once.

auxiliary storage   processor   keyboard   file   command

monitor   user responses   main memory   printers

2. All input is processed in _____ .

3. Computer programs are typically entered via _____ input and saved

   on _____ .

4. After saving computer programs on auxiliary storage, they may typically be recalled or transferred back into

   main memory by a _____ .

5. Commands can be entered via _____ input.

6. A user can enter responses by using a _____ .

7. Data entered to an application is routed to the computer's _____ .

THE KEYBOARD

Fill in the blanks in the following question. Choose your answers from the following.

terminal   personal computer   printer   scanner

1. A user can input data by using a keyboard attached to a _____ , which is in turn

   attached to a mainframe and/or a _____ , which can be stand-alone.

Questions 2-7 pertain to the typical personal computer keyboard. Choose your answers from the following.

function keys   insert key   delete key   cursor control keys   number keys   shift key

numeric keypad   arrow keys   special characters   spacebar   control key   escape key

2. _____ are located above the alphabetic keys and can be used to type in numeric data.

3. _____ are keys that are not numeric and not alphabetic but are required in almost all applications.

4. The _____ is a collection of number keys, the + and − signs, and the decimal point. It is designed for fast input of numeric data.

5. _____ or _____ are used to control the movement of the cursor.

6. By using the _____ and the _____ , you can add or remove characters from a string of characters.

7. The _____ can be used for special purpose actions. These keys are typically found at the left end of the keyboard or at the top of the keyboard.

TERMINALS

1. List the three types of terminals. Choose your answers from the following.

   special purpose   engineering   scientific   dumb   intelligent   CAD/CAM

   _____   _____

   _____

Fill in the answers to the following statements about terminals. Choose your answers from the following.

downloading   independent   processing   printing   dependent

programmable   point of sale   special purpose   uploading

Dumb Terminals

2. A dumb terminal does not perform _____ processing, as all the processing takes place in an external processor.

Intelligent Terminals

3. Intelligent terminals contain _____ capabilities and are sometimes called

_____ terminals.

4. When data moves from an intelligent terminal to an external processing capability, this activity is called data

_____ .

Special Purpose Terminals

5. A _____ terminal maintains sales records, updates inventory, calculates sales tax,

verifies credit, and performs other sales transaction activities.

OTHER INPUT DEVICES

The Mouse

1. The input device below is a _____ .

2. An advantage of the mouse is _____ .

3. The disadvantages of the mouse include _____ and _____ .

Touch Screens

4. Screens that use infrared light beams to identify an input point are called _____ .

5. Touch screens have two advantages. They are a _____ method

and provide _____ .

6. The disadvantages of touch screens include _____ and _____ .

Graphic Input Devices

7-9. Identify these graphic input devices. Choose your answers from the following.

scanner   light pen   graphics tablet   touch screen   digitizer   mouse

_____ (7)

_____ (8)

_____ (9)

Voice Input

10. _____ input allows the user to speak directly to the application using verbal

commands and responses.

11. One advantage of voice input is _____ .

INPUT DEVICES DESIGNED FOR SPECIFIC PURPOSES

1. List the five major types of scanners.

_____   _____

_____   _____

_____

2. List two advantages that input devices have when they are designed for specific purposes.

_____   _____

USER INTERFACES

1. A user interface is the combination of _____ and _____

that allows a user to _____ with a computer system.

Fill in the blanks about the objectives of a user interface. Choose your answers from the following.

saturate   control   respond to   process   information   data

The typical user interface will:

2. _____ messages from the computer

3. _____ the computer

4. request _____ from the computer

EVOLUTION OF USER INTERFACE SOFTWARE

Complete the statements below about the evolution of user interface software. Choose your answers from the following.   menus   difficult   programmers   easy   alternatives

ergonomic   operators   users   prompts

1. Early user interfaces were designed primarily for _____ and

_____ and didn't pay attention to the typical end user.

2. The early use of terminals was characterized by software that was _____ to use.

3. Software that used _____ with data editing allowed users to respond to specific

requests for data from the user.

4. Much of data entry involves the choosing of _____ .

5. _____ are displays on the screen that allow a user to make a selection from

multiple alternatives.

The following questions are designed to familiarize you with the important concept of menus. Complete these

activities.

6-13. Look at this menu and answer the questions. Choose your answers from the following.

```
HyperGraphics: Object  Selection

        Box
        Circle
        Arc
        Line
        Draw
        Fill
        Text
        Animation
        Cut
        End

Enter Selection:___
```

menu prompt   alphabetic
menu title   sequential number
reverse video   menu selection
icon   alphanumeric
mobile   cursor positioning

6. The portion of the menu above the first line is called the _____ .

7. The portion of the menu between the two lines is called the _____ .

8. The portion of the menu below the bottom line is called the _____ .

9. If the menu selection portion of the menu is labeled with numeric items, the selection approach is called

_____ selection.

10. If the menu selection portion of the menu is labeled with alphabetic labels, the selection approach is called

_____ selection.

11. If the menu selection portion of the menu has a movable cursor, the selection approach is called

_____ selection.

12. If you use a movable reverse image to make a selection, the selection approach is called

_____ selection.

13. If you have graphic images available for the selection, the selection approach is called

_____ selection.

14. List three advantages of menus.

_____

_____

_____

15. List a disadvantage of menus.

_____

FEATURES OF A USER INTERFACE

1. Match the following major features of a user interface in the left column with associated characteristics in

the right column.

Features of a user interface

system responses to the user _____

screen design _____

user responses _____

error recovery _____

control and security _____

Component of features

a. password

b. uncluttered

c. simple

d. user told how to recover

e. response time

DATA ENTRY FOR INTERACTIVE AND BATCH PROCESSING

Complete the statements below. Choose your answers from the following.

online   input   offline data entry   output   online data entry   offline

  1. Data entered in the interactive processing mode generates immediate _____ .

  2. Data entry for interactive processing is said to be _____ .

  3. Data for batch processing can be entered in either an _____ or an

    _____ manner.

AN EXAMPLE OF ONLINE DATA ENTRY

Consider the screen and answer the following questions. Choose your answers from the following.

protected fields   prompt   input field   record   unprotected field

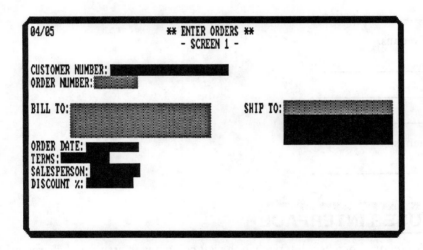

  1. CUSTOMER NUMBER: is an example of a _____ .

  2. The box to the right of ORDER DATE: is an example of a _____ .

  3. The fields to the right of ORDER NUMBER:, BILL TO:, and SHIP TO: are

    called _____ .

ERGONOMICS

1. Match the following ergonomic considerations in the left column with the appropriate characteristic in the right column.

screen angle   _____   a. 80 to 120 degrees

screen   _____   b. 20 to 26 inches

viewing angle   _____   c. antiglare

viewing distance   _____   d. plus or minus 7 degrees

elbow angle   _____   e. 10 to 20 degrees

REVIEW

1. When input is entered into the computer it is placed initially into _____ .

    a. auxiliary storage   d. computer tapes

    b. main memory   e. an output buffer

    c. the CRT

2. Commands are key words and phrases that are entered by the _____ .

    a. computer hardware   d. auxiliary storage

    b. main memory   e. CPU

    c. user

3. User responses refer to the data that a user inputs in response to a question or message from the _____ .

    a. input device   d. source document

    b. output device   e. computer program

    c. main memory

4. A _____ is a symbol that indicates where on the screen the next character entered will be displayed.

    a. cursor   d. caret

    b. tab   e. rectangle

    c. control character

5. Keys that move the cursor symbol on the computer screen are called cursor control keys

   or _____ .

    a. movement keys   d. arrow keys

    b. function keys   e. pointer keys

    c. numeric keys

6. _____ can be programmed to accomplish certain tasks that will assist the user.

    a. Help keys   d. Control keys

    b. Assist keys   e. Function keys

    c. Arrow keys

7. T   F   A dumb terminal has no independent processing capability.

8. Intelligent terminals are also known as _____ terminals.

    a. processing   d. intellectual

    b. control   e. programmable

    c. data

9. A _____ terminal allows data to be entered at the time and place a transaction

   with a customer occurs.

    a. dynamic   d. end user

    b. graphics   e. portable

    c. point of sale

10. T   F   The only function of a mouse is to move the cursor quickly on the terminal screen.

11. A major disadvantage of a touch screen is that the _____ of the touching area is

    not precise.

    a. resolution   d. instrumentation

    b. color   e. coordination

    c. depth

12. Light pens, digitizers, and graphics tablets are examples of _____ _____ input devices.

    a. inexpensive   d. graphic

    b. portable   e. point of sale

    c. expensive

13. Voice input is achieved by creating _____ patterns for words and storing these patterns in auxiliary storage.

    a. repeated   d. digital

    b. several   e. video

    c. audio

14. The magnetic ink character recognition (MICR) input device is used almost exclusively in the _____ industry.

    a. automobile   d. retail

    b. banking   e. computer

    c. manufacturing

15. Scanners are devices that read _____ codes, characters, or images and convert them into a computer format.

    a. printed   d. raised

    b. nonnumeric   e. medical

    c. alphabetic

16. OCR stands for _____ .

    a. optional card reader   d. octal character recognition

    b. our computer reader   e. optical character reader

    c. optical cash register

17. Optical mark readers (OMR) are frequently used in which of the following applications?

    a. desktop publishing input   d. banking transactions

    b. test scoring   e. commercial real estate

    c. capturing customer data

18. A laser scanner is often used by modern _____ to scan and read special bar codes.

    a. automobile dealerships   d. manufacturing plants

    b. grocery stores   e. computer dealers

    c. restaurants

19. Desktop publishing systems will frequently use _____ to convert images into computer format.

    a. laser scanners   d. matrix printers

    b. page scanners   e. OCR devices

    c. image processors

20. When an actual image of a document is required to be captured, _____ will be used.

    a. image processing systems   d. laser adapted optics

    b. filing systems   e. digital/video readers (D/VR)

    c. optical imaging

21. _____ devices are designed to obtain data at the site of the transaction.

    a. Data collection   d. Video collection

    b. External collection   e. Offline collection

    c. Magnetic recording

22. A _____ provides the means for communication between an information system and the user.

    a. CPU   d. user interface

    b. disk drive   e. graphics terminal

    c. modem

23. In most instances the _____ determines the ultimate quality of the user interface.

    a. computer size   d. computer speed

    b. terminal quality   e. software

    c. number of colors

24. One of the first steps in improving the user interface was the utilization of _____ on the screen.

    a. prompts   d. graphical images

    b. terse imperatives   e. commands

    c. extensive directions

25. _____ were implemented to assist the end user with the selection of alternatives.

    a. Choices   d. Options

    b. Prompts   e. Menus

    c. Directories

26. Sequential number, alphabetic selection, cursor positioning, and reverse video are examples
    of _____ .

    a. prompt selection alternatives   d. menu headers

    b. menu selection alternatives   e. menu directions

    c. user alternatives

27. When icon selection is used for identifying a user alternative, the choice is identified
    by a _____ .

    a. special function key   d. character alternative

    b. textual prompt   e. menu of menus

    c. graphic image

28. _____ are those messages and actions taken by the computer when a user enters
    data into the computer.

    a. System responses   d. Menu headers

    b. Menu selection alternatives   e. Menu directions

    c. User alternatives

29. _____ is the elapsed time between the instant a user enters data and the instant
    the computer responds.

    a. Time between prompts   d. Response time

    b. Menu selection time   e. System selection time

    c. Data entry time

30. A _____ is a value, such as a word or number, that identifies a user to the
    information system.

    a. character ID   d. user program

    b. unique identifier   e. system tag

    c. password

31. T   F   In offline data entry, the device that stores the data that is entered is not connected to the computer.

32. A common method for data entry is to use _____ to identify input fields to the
    data entry operator.

    a. prompt characters   d. windowing

    b. numeric codes   e. touch screens

    c. reverse video

33. Entering data from various locations in an organization is called _____ .

    a. external data entry   d. distributed data entry

    b. remote data entry   e. production data entry

    c. centralized data entry

34. Which of the following would be of concern if you were considering the ergonomics of a situation?

    a. screen height   c. menu type

    b. user responses   d. response time

35. _____ is the amount of data entered for a given time period.

    a. Data entry speed   d. Transaction processing

    b. Transaction volume   e. Data flow processing

    c. Flow of data

36. A _____ error occurs when an error is made in copying the values from a source document.

    a. transposition   d. transcription

    b. numeric   e. computer

    c. critical

Chapter 5

The Processor Unit

Objectives

1. Identify the components of the processor unit and describe their use.
2. Define a bit and describe how a series of bits in a byte is used to represent characters.
3. Discuss how the ASCII and EBCDIC codes represent characters.
4. Describe why the binary and hexadecimal numbering systems are used with computer systems.
5. List and describe the four steps in a machine cycle.
6. Discuss the three primary factors that affect the speed of the processor unit.
7. Describe the characteristics of RAM and ROM memory. List several other types of memory.
8. Describe the process of manufacturing integrated circuits.

Chapter Outline

WHAT IS THE PROCESSOR UNIT?

1-2. In the following illustration of a processor unit, identify which part represents the memory and which part represents the central processing unit.

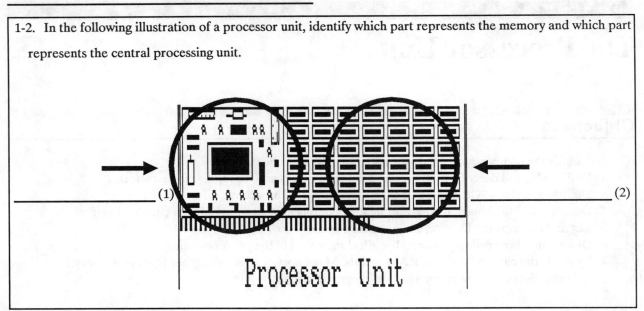

The Central Processing Unit

Complete these two statements. Choose your answers from the following.

control unit   main memory   arithmetic/logic unit   central processing unit

3. The brain within a human being is analogous to the _____ within the

computer system.

4. The two major subunits within the CPU are the _____

and _____ .

5-10. Fill in the major functions of the control unit and the arithmetic/logic unit in the illustration below.

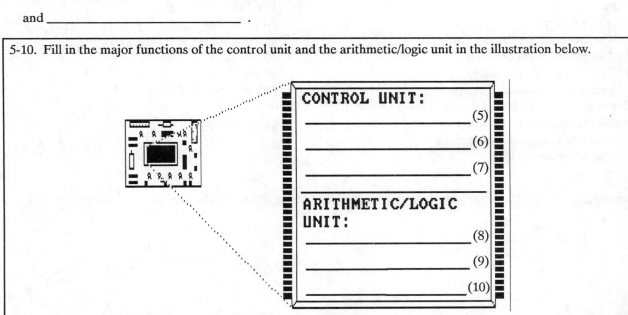

Main Memory

11-13. Complete the following illustration of main memory within the processor unit.

Main Memory

OPERATING SYSTEM	APPLICATION PROGRAM	
		Data
	(11)	(12) (13)

14-18. Complete these statements. Choose your answers from the following.

megabyte   value   byte   address

512   nibble   640   nanobyte   gigabyte   value   1024

14. Each location within main memory has a _____ .

15. One _____ can be stored or retained at each location in main memory.

16. One kilobyte (KB) equals _____ bytes.

17. The average PC will have a memory capacity of _____ KB.

18. One thousand KB equal a(n) _____ , and one million KB equal

   a _____ .

HOW PROGRAMS AND DATA ARE REPRESENTED IN MEMORY

Complete the following two statements about data in memory.

1. The three classifications of characters are alphabetic, _____ ,

   and _____ .

2. Within memory, a character equals one _____ .

Show how the following characters would be represented in memory locations.

3. John Doe

4. $123.69

Complete the following statements about binary numbers and character representations within memory.

5. A byte is equal to _____ binary digits.

6. Binary digits is another way of saying _____ .

7. A bit can be either ◯ = _____ or ● = _____ .

8. The following number is called a _____ number.

   0 1 0 1 0 0 1

9. American Standard Code for Information Interchange, abbreviated as _____ , is

   a method for representing characters in memory.

10. EBCDIC is another method for representing _____ in memory.

11. Binary representation is restricted to the representation of powers of the number _____ .

PARITY

Complete these statements about parity. Choose your answers from the following.

data   error   transmission   left   odd   right   even   information

1. The parity bit is an additional bit that is added to the _____ end of a memory

   location or byte.

2. _____ parity implies that the sum of the bits (including the parity bit) that are on

   will equal an odd number.

3. _____ parity implies that the sum of the bits (including the parity bit) that are on

   will equal an even number.

4. Parity is typically used for _____ detection during the movement or transmission of bytes of data.

5. In this example the parity bits are the same, both off, and the parity is _____ .

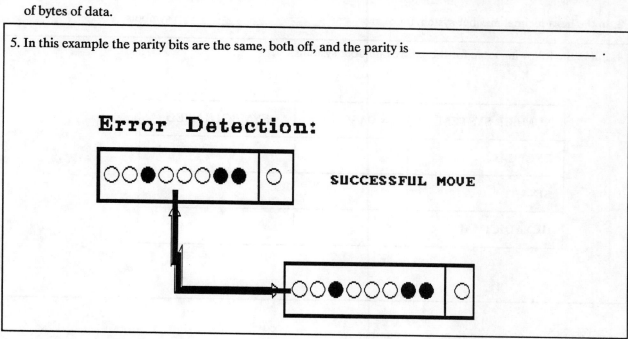

6. In this example a _____ error has occurred, and the parity bit from the original location disagrees with the parity bit of the destination location.

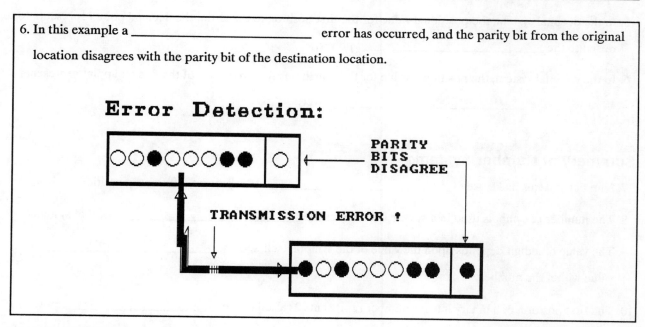

NUMBER SYSTEMS

Complete the following statements.

1. In the decimal number system there are _____ symbols.

2. In the binary number system there are _____ symbols.

3. In the hexadecimal number system there are _____ symbols.

4. Fill in the following table for these three number systems.

NUMBER SYSTEM	BASE	SYMBOLS USED
DECIMAL		
BINARY		
HEXADICIMAL		

Complete the following questions about number systems.

5. In the decimal system, the positional value for the first position to the left of the decimal point represents 10 raised to the _____ power.

6. In the decimal system, the positional value for the fourth position to the left of the decimal point represents 10 raised to the _____ power.

Summary of Number Systems

7. Number systems make use of _____ to represent different quantities.

8. The number of symbols used in a system determines the _____ of that system.

9. The value of a digit depends upon the value of the symbol itself and its _____ value within the number.

10. The first position of a binary integer number represents 2 raised to the _____ power.

11. The third position of a binary integer number represents a value of _____ .

12. What is the decimal equivalent of the following binary number?

    1 0 1 1 0 = _____

13. The second position of a hexadecimal integer number represents 16 raised to the

_____ power.

14. What is the decimal equivalent of the following hexadecimal number?

   1 2 A C F = _____

15. In converting from binary to hexadecimal and hexadecimal to binary, each hexadecimal digit is represented

   by _____ binary digits.

16. Fill in the equivalent numbers.

	Equivalent Base 2 Number			Equivalent Base 16 Number
5	_____		1100	_____
A	_____		1011	_____

17. Convert the following binary number to hexadecimal.

   1 0 1 0 1 1 0 0 = _____

HOW THE PROCESSOR UNIT EXECUTES PROGRAMS AND MANIPULATES DATA

Machine Language Instructions

Fill in the blanks in the following two statements.

1. _____ instructions are the instructions that the processor unit executes.

2. The _____ of the instruction specifies the operation that the instruction is to

   perform.

3-4. Fill in the missing portions of a typical machine language instruction.

Operation Code	_____ (3)	Value 1 Address	_____ (4)

The Machine Cycle

5. List the four parts of the machine cycle.

_____   _____

_____   _____

6. The fetch and decode phase of the machine cycle is called the _____ cycle.

7. The execute and store phase of the machine cycle is called the _____ cycle.

PROCESSOR SPEEDS

Complete these statements. Choose your answers from the following.

kilohertz   MIPS   megahertz   length   bus   width   port

1. The unit of measurement for the processor speed is _____ .

2. The execution rate of instructions is measured in _____ .

3. The _____ is the transmission path for data flow among the various components of the computer system.

4. The _____ of the bus determines how much data can flow among the various components.

5. Fill in the number of transfers in the table below.

Buses:

BUS WIDTH	TRANSFER SIZE (IN BITS)		
	8	16	32
8			
16			
32			
	NUMBER OF TRANSFERS		

Complete these statements regarding various processor capabilities. Choose your answers from the following.

twelve   640   one   two   sixteen   four   512

6. An eight-bit processor can operate on _____ byte(s) of data at a time.

7. A 16-bit processor can operate on _____ byte(s) of data at the same time.

8. A 32-bit processor can operate on _____ byte(s) of data at the same time.

9. An eight-bit processor can address up to _____ KB of memory.

10. A 16-bit processor can address up to _____ MB of memory.

11. A 30-bit processor can address up to _____ MB of memory.

ARCHITECTURE OF PROCESSOR UNITS

1. The design of the processor can range from a single board to _____ boards.

2. List two special purposes that a coprocessor can have.

_____   _____

3. In _____ processing several program instructions may be executed at the same time in multiple processing units.

4. In _____ technology there is a subset of instructions that are frequently used that comprise the instruction set.

TYPES OF MEMORY

Complete these statements. Choose your answers from the following.

transistors   ROM   vacuum tubes   core   RAM   semiconductor

1. _____ were the earliest physical devices used for memory operations.

2. With _____ memory the speed of computers reached the microsecond range, while _____ memory took the speed to the nanosecond range.

3. In _____ , memory is erased when power is removed.

4. In _____ no data is lost when power is removed.

REVIEW

1. The central processing unit (CPU) is comprised of two primary units, the arithmetic/logic unit and the _____ unit.

   a. memory   d. files

   b. control   e. function

   c. operating

2. In addition to the central processing unit (CPU), the processor unit also contains the computer's _____ .

   a. "brain"

   b. main memory

   c. input devices

           d. output devices

           e. disk drives

3. Sixteen kilobytes (16 KB) is approximately how many bytes?

   a. 1.6 million

   b. 16

   c. 166,000

           d. 16,000

           e. 1.6 billion

4. How many bytes are required to represent the following series of symbols (number/special characters)?

_____ @123.(456)

   a. six

   b. seven

   c. eight

           d. nine

           e. ten

5. If a ● represents an OFF condition and a ○ represents an ON condition, what is the binary equivalent of the following storage locations?

```
●○●○○●●○
```

   a. 1 0 1 0 0 1 1 0

   b. 0 1 1 0 1 0 0 1

   c. 0 1 0 1 1 0 0 1

           d. 1 0 1 0 0 1 0 1

           e. 0 1 0 1 1 0 1 0

6. _____ is the most widely used character coding system for microcomputers.

   a. ASCII

   b. EBCDIC

   c. Packed decimal

           d. Zoned decimal

           e. Decimal

7. For an odd parity system, what is the value of the parity bit for 01101001?

   a. 1

   b. 0

   c. 5

           d. 4

           e. none of the above

8. The _____ of a number system indicates how many symbols are used in it.

    a. position

    b. exponent

    c. digit

    d. base

    e. sum

9. In a binary number system, what is the value of the indicated position? 0 $\boxed{1}$ 1 0

    a. 2^3

    b. 2^2

    c. 2^1

    d. 2^0

    e. 0

10. In the hexadecimal number system a 16-bit binary number can be represented by _____ hexadecimal digits.

    a. 8

    b. 2

    c. 3

    d. 4

    e. 6

11. A machine language instruction usually consists of three parts: the _____ , the data length(s), and the memory addresses of the data.

    a. CPU address

    b. operation code

    c. instruction set

    d. CPU data

    e. none of the above

12. Collectively, the steps fetch instruction, execute instruction, decode instruction, and store results are called the _____ .

    a. execution cycle

    b. instruction cycle

    c. machine cycle

    d. information cycle

    e. none of the above

13. The processing speed of computers is often compared in _____ .

    a. chips

    b. bus width

    c. address range

    d. MIPS

    e. none of the above

14. For a computer incorporating a 16-bit bus, how many data transfers are required to move 8 bytes of memory?

    a. 4

    b. 1

    c. 2

    d. 8

    e. 16

15. The amount of memory that a CPU can efficiently access is primarily determined by

the _____ .

    a. system clock   d. processor speed

    b. bus width   e. character codes

    c. word size

16. A specialized processor designed to perform a specific task (such as numeric processing) in conjunction

with the CPU is called a _____ .

    a. RISC processor   d. perpendicular processor

    b. bus processor   e. none of the above

    c. coprocessor

17. Currently, the most prevalent technology used to implement primary memory

is _____ .

    a. RISC   d. EPROM

    b. core   e. semiconductor

    c. vacuum tube

18. RAM is said to be _____ , because the programs and data stored are erased

when power to the computer is turned off.

    a. volatile   d. programmable

    b. static   e. read only

    c. erasable

Chapter 6

Output From the Computer

Objectives

1. Define the term output.
2. List the common types of reports and graphs that are used for output.
3. Describe the classifications of printers.
4. List the types of printers used with personal computers and describe how they work.
5. Discuss the quality of output obtainable from various types of printers.
6. Describe printers used for large computers.
7. Describe the types of screens available and list common screen features.
8. List and describe other types of output devices used with computers.

Chapter Outline

What Is Output?
Common Types of Output
  Reports
  Graphics
Printers
  How Are Printers Classified?
    Impact and Nonimpact
    Speed
  Printer Features
    Carriage Size
    Feed Mechanism
    Bidirectional Printing
Printers for Small and Medium Computers
  Dot Matrix Printers
  Daisy Wheel Printers
  Thermal Printers
  Ink Jet Printers
  Laser Printers
Printers for Large Computers
  Chain Printers
  Band Printers
  High-Speed Laser Printers

Screens
  Screen Features
    Size
    Color
    Cursor
    Scrolling
    Paging
    Other Screen Features
  Types of Screens
  How Characters Are Displayed on a Screen
    How Color Is Produced
    How Flat Panel Displays Work
Other Output Devices
  Plotters
  Computer Output Microfilm
  Voice Output
Summary of Output From the Computer

WHAT IS OUTPUT?

1. Output is data that has been processed into a useful form called _____ .

COMMON TYPES OF OUTPUT

1-2. Correctly label the form of output that the people are looking at in the two diagrams below. Choose your answers from the following.   terminal   hard copy   soft copy   printing

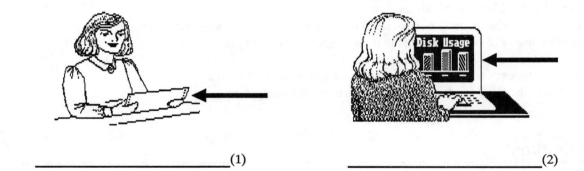

_____(1)   _____(2)

Reports

Complete these statements regarding reports. Choose your answers from the following.

Information   Internal reports   External reports   Reports   Documents

3. _____ represent information presented in an organized form.

4. _____ are those reports used by individuals within an organization.

5. _____ are those reports used by individuals outside the organization.

6-8. Classify the three examples of reports below.

```
      UNITS SOLD REPORT                      SALES BY DEPARTMENT              INVENTORY EXCEPTION REPORT

                          QTY                         UNITS                 ITEM        ITEM        QUANTITY
DEPT DEPT NAME    ITEM DESCRIPTION SOLD   DEPT DEPT NAME     SOLD   SALES $   NO.     DESCRIPTION     ON HAND

 10  MENS FURNISHINGS 105  T-SHIRT    3    10  MENS FURNISHINGS 130   653.35   105      T-SHIRT          24
 10  MENS FURNISHINGS 109  SOCKS    127    12  SLEEPWEAR          6   189.70   125      SCARF             3
 12  SLEEPWEAR        199  ROBE       6    14  MENS ACCESSORIES   4    98.00   126      BELT             17
```

_____(6)   _____(7)   _____(8)

Graphics

9. _____ output displays information in the form of charts, graphs, or pictures, assisting in analyzing and understanding data quickly and easily.

10-12. Label the three types of graphics displayed below.

Regional Sales

_____(10)

Sales - 7/11-7/15

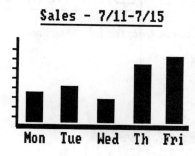

_____(11)

1st Quarter Revenue

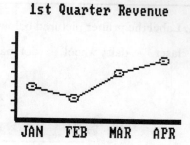

_____(12)

PRINTERS

1. The two types of impact printers are _____ striking and

_____ striking printers.

2. _____ printing occurs without having a mechanism strike the paper.

3-6. Fill in the following table.

Speed Classification of Printer	
Speed Type	Speed Description
(3)	prints one character at a time (15-600 characters per second)
(4)	prints a line at a time (300-600 lines per minute)
(5)	prints a line at a time (600-3,000 lines per minute)
(6)	prints a page at a time (3,000-20,000 lines per minute)

7. The standard carriage size for printers is 8 1/2 inches or _____ characters per line.

8. The wide carriage is 14 inches or _____ characters per line.

9. The two types of feed mechanisms for printers are _____ feed

   and _____ feed.

10. A _____ printer can print in both directions.

PRINTERS FOR SMALL AND MEDIUM COMPUTERS

1. Label the printer pictured below. Choose from the following answers.

   laser   daisy wheel   dot matrix   chain

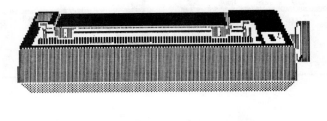

_____

2-4. Label the components in the figure below. Choose from the following answers.

   printing head   printing chain   paper   ribbon   laser

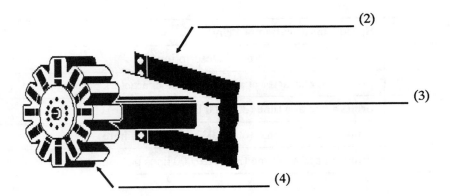

5. The fewest number of pins a dot matrix printer can have is _____ pins.

6. The letter E in the figure at the right is in _____ print.

   Choose your answer from these.   bold   standard   italicized

7. The letter E in the figure at the right is in _____ print.

   Choose your answer from these.   bold   condensed   enlarged

8. Dot matrix printers can print text and _____ .

9. The diagram below represents a _____ printer.

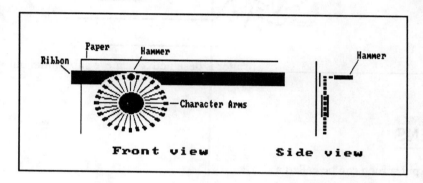

10. The _____ printer uses heat to produce output.

11. The _____ printer uses a nozzle to spray liquid ink drops to produce output.

12. The _____ printer works like a photocopy machine and supports desktop

   publishing.

PRINTERS FOR LARGE COMPUTERS

1-5. Label the components of the chain printer in the figure below. Choose your answers from the following.

   chain   hammers   paper   ribbon   drive gear   printer slug   daisy wheel

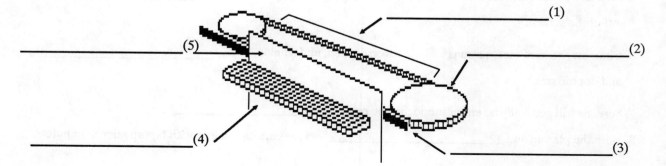

6-10. Label the diagram of the chain and band printer below. Choose your answers from the following.

chain band   printer slug   hammer   scalloped steel print band   paper   ribbon   magnet

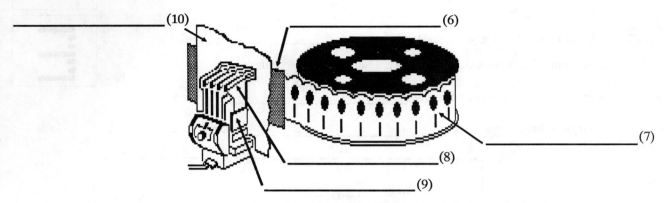

_____(10)   _____(6)

_____(7)

_____(8)

_____(9)

11. The _____ printer is designed to achieve substantial output speed.

SCREENS

1. The output screen can be called a _____ , a _____ ,

   or a _____ .

Complete these statements about screens. Choose your answers from the following.

pixels   color   medium resolution   underline   cursor

80   blinking   LCD   scroll   higher resolution   monochrome

2. The typical output screen has a capacity of 25 lines of _____ characters.

3. The_____ is a marker on the screen that identifies where on the screen the next

   character will be entered.

4. A cursor can appear as a(n) _____ , a(n) _____ ,

   or a(n) _____ .

5. As a line of data is placed on the last line of the screen, the topmost line will _____

   off of the screen.

6. Characteristics of most screens include reverse video, underlining, bold, _____ ,

   and double size.

7. Screens will generally be either monochrome or _____ .

8. Both the plasma and _____ screens are associated with laptop microcomputers.

9. Each screen is composed of many small units that can be illuminated, which are

called _____ .

10. _____ screens have smaller pixels and, therefore, higher quality graphic output.

11. _____ screens use three electron guns to produce color output.

OTHER OUTPUT DEVICES

1. Label the output device shown below.

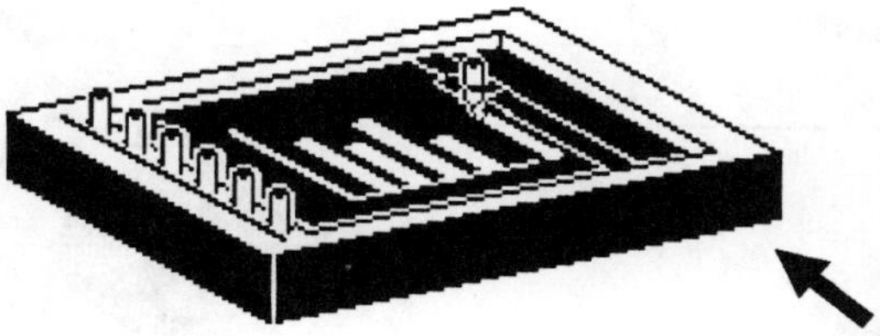

_____ (1)

2. List three types of plotters.

_____

_____

_____

3. _____ can record information on microfiche or 16mm, 35mm, or 105mm roll film.

4. _____ can be recorded, stored, and played back to produce audio output.

5. A _____ can transform words stored in main memory into human speech.

REVIEW

1. _____ is data that has been processed into a useful form called information.

    a. A computer program   c. Output

    b. Printed reports   d. Graphics

2. The two most common types of output are _____ .

    a. reports and graphics   c. hard copy and soft copy

    b. computer screens and printers   d. computer programs and computer screens

3. An _____ report should have a high quality print output because it is used by individuals outside the organization.

    a. internal   b. external

4. Each line on a _____ report usually corresponds to one input record.

    a. summary

    b. detail

    c. exception

5. Computer _____ are used to present information so it can be quickly and easily understood.

    a. screens   c. graphics

    b. output   d. reports

6. The following graphic is an example of a _____ .

    a. pie chart

    b. bar chart

    c. line graph

7. The following graphic is an example of a _____ .

    a. pie chart

    b. bar chart

    c. line graph

8. Printers are classified as being either _____ .

    a. low speed or high speed   c. impact or nonimpact

    b. small or large   d. graphic or letter quality

9. The printing rate for medium- and high-speed printers is stated as the number of _____ per minute.

    a. characters   c. lines

    b. pages   d. forms

10. Printer features include _____ .

    a. carriage size   c. bidirectional printing

    b. feed mechanism   d. all of the above

11. The standard carriage size is _____ inches.

12. Two types of printer feed mechanisms are _____ .

   a. tractor feed and continuous flow   c. tractor feed and friction feed

   b. continuous flow and sprockets   d. none of the above

13. _____ printers have small pins that are contained in a print head.

   a. Daisy wheel   c. Band

   b. Dot matrix   d. Chain

14. The _____ printer prints fully formed characters for letter quality output.

   a. daisy wheel   c. band

   b. dot matrix   d. ink jet

15. Thermal printers use _____ to produce fully formed characters.

16. A _____ printer is a nonimpact printer that operates in a manner similar to a copying machine.

   a. ink jet   c. chain

   b. laser   d. band

17. _____ printers have interchangeable bands with many different styles of fonts.

18. Large high-speed printers are often called _____ printers.

   a. super   c. page

   b. fast   d. chain

19. Which of the following is not a type of screen?

   a. color   d. plasma

   b. monochrome   e. LCD

   c. scrolling

20. Laptop computers use a special display device called _____ , using a polarizing material to form images upon the screen.

   a. CRT -- cathode ray tube   c. COM -- computer output microfilm

   b. LCD -- liquid crystal display d. VDT -- video display terminal

21. Which output device would most likely be used in an architectural, engineering, or design firm?

   a. chain printer   c. plotter

   b. daisy wheel printer   d. microfiche

22. T   F   Computer output microfilm (COM) records microscopic images on roll or sheet film.

Chapter 7

Auxiliary Storage

Objectives

1. Define auxiliary storage.
2. Identify the primary devices used for personal computer auxiliary storage.
3. Describe the manner in which data is stored on disks.
4. Describe the methods used to back up data stored on floppy and hard disks.
5. Identify the types of disk storage used with large computers.
6. Explain how tape storage is used with large computers.
7. List and describe three other forms of auxiliary storage: optical, solid state, and mass storage.

Chapter Outline

What Is Auxiliary Storage?
Auxiliary Storage for Personal Computers
  Floppy Disks
    How Is a Floppy Disk Formatted?
    Hard- and Soft-Sectored Diskettes
    What Is the Storage Capacity of a Floppy
     Disk?
    How Is Data Stored on a Floppy Disk?
    What Is Access Time?
    The Care of Floppy Disks
  Hard Disks
    What Is a Fixed Disk?
    How Is Data Stored on a Hard Disk?
    Disk Cartridges
  Protecting Data Stored on a Disk
    How Is the Write-Protect Notch Used?
    Backup Storage
    Cartridge Tape

Auxiliary Storage for Medium and Large
  Computers
  Magnetic Disks
    Fixed Disks
    Removable Disks
    How Is Data Physically Organized on a Disk?
  Magnetic Tape
    Reel-to-Reel Tape Devices
    Cartridge Tape Devices
    How Is Data Stored on Magnetic Tape?
Other Forms of Auxiliary Storage
  Optical Storage Technology
  Solid-State Devices
  Mass Storage Devices
Summary of Auxiliary Storage

WHAT IS AUXILIARY STORAGE?

1. Fill in the blank. Choose your answer from the following.

   volatile   nonvolatile   static   dynamic

   Auxiliary storage is _____ program and data storage.

2. List two example auxiliary storage devices.

   _____   _____

3. Auxiliary storage is an _____ device capable of receiving output from the

   computer and/or sending input to the computer.

4. Fill in the typical storage requirements of the entities below. Choose your answers from the following.

   gigabytes   magnabytes   kilobytes   megabytes   nanobytes

   Personal User _____

   Small Business _____

   Large Business _____

AUXILIARY STORAGE FOR PERSONAL COMPUTERS

Floppy Disks

1. List three characteristics of floppy disk auxiliary storage.

   _____

   _____

   _____

2. What are the physical dimensions of the two most commonly used floppy disks? Choose your answers from

   the following.   8   3 1/4   5 1/4   3 1/2   5 1/2

   _____ inches

   _____ inches

3-4. Label the 5 1/4 inch disk below, providing the names of the material of which the disk is made and with which it is coated.

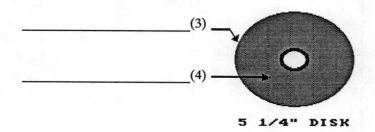

_____(3)

_____(4)

5 1/4" DISK

5. The 5 1/4 inch disk fits into a _____ .

6. List two parts of the disk jacket.

_____   _____

7. The 3 1/2 inch disk has a _____ cover.

8. When you format a floppy disk you are defining the disk's _____

   and _____ .

9-10. Label the floppy disk below, specifying which is a track and which is a sector.

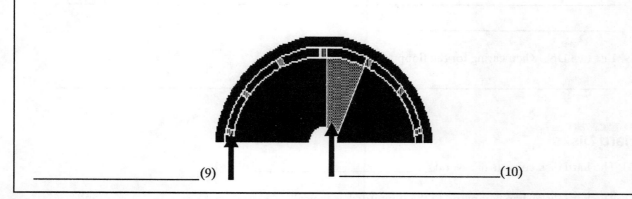

_____(9)   _____(10)

11. Fill in the table below concerning the format of the floppy disk.

DISKETTE TYPE	TRACKS PER DISK	SECTORS PER TRACK	TRACK NUMBERING
5 1/4"			
3 1/2"			

12. The hard-sectored disk has _____ holes and a fixed

_____ size.

13. The soft-sectored disk has an _____ hole and software-defined

_____ size.

14. The three factors that determine the storage capacity of the floppy disk are:

_____

_____

_____

15. In order to record and read a double-sided disk, the physical mechanism must have

_____ read/write heads.

16. The recording density of the floppy disk is measured in _____ per inch.

17. List the four factors that determine access time.

_____   _____

_____   _____

18. List five Don'ts when caring for the floppy disk.

_____   _____

_____   _____

_____

19. List two Do's when caring for the floppy disk.

_____   _____

Hard Disks

20. The hard disk consists of several _____ of disks.

21. The hard disk when compared to the floppy disk is typically _____ and

_____ .

22. The fixed disk is permanently _____ in a _____ case.

23. Label the following type of fixed disk.

_____ (23)

24-27. Label this diagram of a hard disk. Choose your answers from the following.

actuators   sectors   plates   spindle   platters   read/write heads   rotator arms

_____ (24)

_____ (26)

(25) _____

_____ (27)

28. The disk head clearance on the hard disk is one _____ of an inch.

29. When the disk head collides with and damages the disk surface, causing the loss of data on the fixed disk, we say that we have a _____ .

30. The capacity range for the 5 1/4 inch hard disk drive is from _____ MB to _____ MB.

31. The access time for the 5 1/4 inch hard disk ranges from _____ milliseconds to _____ milliseconds.

32. List three advantages of the hard disk auxiliary storage device. Choose your answers from the following.

easily backed up   online storage   large capacity   faster access   more reliable

_____

_____

_____

33. List four characteristics of the disk cartridge. Choose your answers from the following.

portable   easily backed up   easily secured   more reliable   fast access   high capacity   cost

_____   _____

_____   _____

Protecting Data Stored on a Disk

34. Circle the write-protect notch on the following disk.

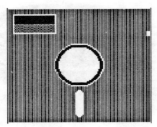

35. On a 5 1/4 inch disk, when the write-protect notch is _____ data may be written,

and when it is _____ data may not be written.

36. A _____ copy is a copy of an original disk that protects the data stored on the

original disk.

AUXILIARY STORAGE FOR MEDIUM AND LARGE COMPUTERS

Magnetic Disk

1. _____ is used as an abbreviation for direct-access storage device.

2. Disks for large computers can be either _____ , which requires them to always

remain intact, or _____ , which allows them to be detached from their cabinets.

3-4. Label the removable disk drive shown below. Choose your answers from the following.

stand-alone cabinet   disk pack   magnetic tape   disk cartridge

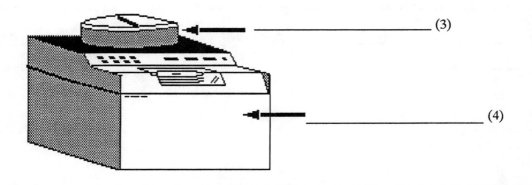

_____ (3)

_____ (4)

5. The range for the removable disk pack is from _____ MB to

_____ MB.

6. The two methods of recording data on the magnetic disk are:

_____   _____

Magnetic Tape

7. List two primary uses of magnetic tape.

_____   _____

8. The magnetic tape reel lengths range from _____ feet up to

_____ feet.

9. One magnetic tape reel can contain up to _____ MB of data or information.

10-13. Label the reel-to-reel tape device shown below.

_____ (10)

_____ (11)

_____ (12)

_____ (13)

14. Data is stored on the magnetic tape using the _____ coding method and using

_____ channels on the tape.

15. The recording density of the magnetic tape ranges from _____ bpi to

_____ bpi.

16. The newer cartridges can hold up to _____ bpi.

17. The space between records on a magnetic tape is referred to as a(n) _____ gap.

18. Blocked records means that several _____ records are grouped into one block.

19. Each block in the blocked record format is referred to as a(n) _____ record.

OTHER FORMS OF AUXILIARY STORAGE

In 1 and 2, complete the statements about optical storage technology. Choose your answers from the following.

trillion   lase   WORM   billion   CDROM   EPROM

1. Optical storage technology uses a 12-inch optical disk capable of storing several

   _____ characters of data and utilizes lasers to burn microscopic holes on the disk.

2. The two major types of optical storage technology are _____

   and _____ .

3. Two other forms of auxiliary storage devices include _____ storage

   devices and _____ storage devices.

REVIEW

1. Auxiliary storage is also known as _____ .

   a. primary storage   c. secondary storage

   b. main storage   d. read-only storage

2. T   F   Auxiliary storage is a volatile storage medium.

3. The _____ inch diskette holds more data than the

   _____ inch diskette.

   a. 5 1/4,   3 1/2   c.   5 1/2, 3 1/2

   b. 3 1/2,   5 1/4   d. 3 1/2,   5 1/2

4. Formatting a diskette involves _____ .

   a. labelling the diskette

   b. defining the capacity of the diskette

   c. labelling the tracks on the diskette surface

   d. defining the tracks and sectors on the diskette surface

5. T   F   The number of sectors on a soft-sectored diskette is determined when a disk is formatted.

6. Which of the following does NOT contribute to the storage capacity of a diskette?

   a. the number of sectors on the disk

   b. the recording density of the bits on a track

   c. the number of tracks on the disk

   d. the number of sides of the disk

7. Recording density refers to the number of _____ .

    a. characters recorded per inch   c. bits recorded per inch

    b. sectors on a track   d. tracks on a disk

8. Access time is comprised of seek time, _____ , settling time, and data transfer rate.

9. Seek time is the time required _____ .

    a. to position the read/write head over the desired record

    b. to position the read/write head over the proper track

    c. to place the read/write head in contact with the disk

    d. for the sector to rotate under the read/write head

10. T F   Hard disks are called fixed disks because the read/write heads do not move; only the platters rotate.

11. T F   Hard disks have slower access time than diskettes because hard disks store larger volumes of data.

12. Disk cartridges provide _____ .

    a. storage and access features of diskettes

    b. less security than hard disks

    c. storage features of a hard disk

    d. the portability of a hard disk

13. Protection of data on a hard drive is accomplished by _____ .

    a. backing up data onto a cartridge tape

    b. covering the write-protect notch

    c. opening the write-protect window

    d. all of the above

14. Which of the following would you NOT expect to find as auxiliary storage on a large computer system?

    a. fixed disks   c. magnetic tape

    b. removable disks   d. hard card

15. The _____ method of organizing data is more efficient because it reduces movement of the read/write heads.

    a. sector   c. track

    b. cylinder   d. sectional

16. T F   The primary uses of magnetic tape are data transfer and backup.

17. Which of the following has the greatest storage capacity?

    a. magnetic tape   c. cartridge tape

    b. 5 1/4 inch diskette   d. hard card

18. A program processes _____ ; auxiliary storage

    transfers _____ .

    a. physical records, logical records

    b. physical records, physical records

    c. logical records, physical records

    d. logical records, logical records

19. Blocking refers to the _____ .

    a. gaps between each block (IBG)

    b. gaps between each record (IRG)

    c. grouping of physical records

    d. grouping of logical records

20. A disadvantage of CDROM is its _____ .

    a. limited storage capacity   c. volatility

    b. inability to be reused   d. use of second-generation technology

21. T F Solid-state storage devices contain no moving parts and provide faster access than conventional disk drives.

22. T F Mass storage devices are NOT useful in large database environments.

Chapter 8

File Organization and Databases

Objectives

1. Describe sequential files, indexed files, and direct (or relative) files.
2. Explain the difference between sequential retrieval and random retrieval of records from a file.
3. Describe the data maintenance procedures for updating files, including adding, changing, and deleting data in a file or database.
4. Discuss the advantages of a database management system (DBMS).
5. Describe a relational database system.
6. Describe a hierarchical database system.
7. Describe a network database system.
8. Explain the use of a query language.
9. Describe the responsibilities of a database administrator.

Chapter Outline

WHAT IS A FILE?

Complete the following statements. Choose your answers from the following.

database   file   fields   data item   header   field

1. A _____ is a collection of related records.

2. A record is a collection of _____ .

3. A _____ is a data item or data element.

TYPES OF FILE ORGANIZATION

1. The three major types of file organization are:

_____

_____

_____

Sequential File Organization

2. Identify two applications for which sequential organization is useful. Choose your answers from the

following.   database applications   printing   backup   payroll

_____   _____

3. In the following illustration of records organized as a sequential file, how many records would you have to

read in order to access the data in record 56? _____

| Record 1 | Record 2 | Record 3 | Record 4 | ... |

| Record 55 | Record 56 | Record 57 | ... |

Indexed File Organization

4. In indexed file organization, the index to the file uses what two items to identify a particular record?

   Choose your answers from the following.

   key field   hash function   disk address   relative record number

   _____   _____

5. Using indexed organization you can access a file in either a sequential manner or a

   _____ manner.

Direct or Relative File Organization

6. In direct file organization you can access a file using direct disk address or using the file's

   _____ position within the file.

7. Another approach for retrieval in direct or relative file organization is the use of a

   _____ formula to produce the relative position number within the file.

Summary of File Organization Concepts

8. Fill in the following table, which summarizes the file processing characteristics of the three file types.

   For those file types that have multiple access methods, place an asterisk next to the *primary* access method.

FILE TYPE	TYPE OF STORAGE	ACCESS METHOD
SEQUENTIAL		
INDEXED		
DIRECT (RELATIVE)		

HOW IS DATA IN FILES MAINTAINED?

1. In order to keep data current, you need to perform three operations on records. These three operations are:

   _____

   _____

   _____

DATABASES: A BETTER WAY TO MANAGE DATA AND INFORMATION

1-2. Consider the two illustrations below. One illustrates multiple separate files -- that is, maintaining separate files for multiple applications. The other illustrates a database -- that is, integrated files. Label the two illustrations.

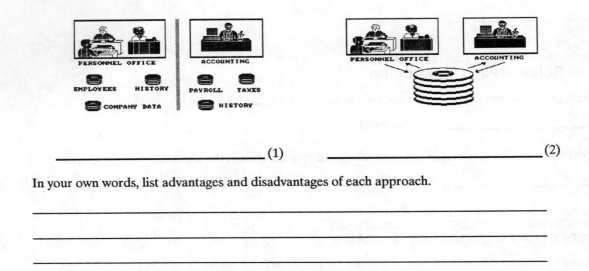

_____ (1)   _____ (2)

In your own words, list advantages and disadvantages of each approach.

_____

_____

_____

WHAT IS A DATABASE?

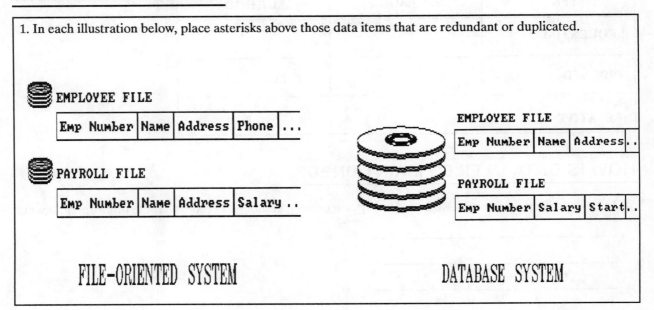

2. The software used to create, maintain, and extract information in the multiple related files of a database is

called a _____ .

3. The software used to create, maintain, and extract information from a single file at a time is called

a _____ .

WHY USE A DATABASE?

1. List four reasons why you would use a database over a file approach. Choose your answers from the

following.   easier to print   improved data integrity   improved data security

faster access time   reduced data redundancy   integrated files

_____   _____

_____   _____

TYPES OF DATABASE ORGANIZATION

1. List the three types of databases. Choose your answers from the following.

network   random   communication   relational   hierarchical   integrated

_____

_____

_____

Relational Database

In items 2-6, complete the statements about the relational approach. Choose your answers from the following.

gate   field   data item   link   record   file   domain   range

2. A table or relation is analogous to the concept of a _____ .

3. A row or tuple is analogous to the concept of _____ .

4. An attribute is analogous to the concept of a _____ .

5. The field label or title (e.g., EMPLOYEE NUMBER) is called a _____ in the

relational approach.

6. A field that is common to more than one relational file is called a _____ .

7. List two advantages of the relational approach.

_____   _____

Hierarchical Database

8. The topmost record in a hierarchical database is called the _____ record.

9. One method of discussing the relationship of records in a hierarchical database is to use the family

relationship approach of _____ - _____ .

10-12. In the illustration below, label the records indicated as to their relationship to each other.   That is, label

which are parent records and which are children records.

```
              ┌──────────────────┐
              │ ABC CORPORATION  │  _____ (10)
              └──────────────────┘
               /                \
    ┌──────────┐                ┌──────────┐
    │ DEPT 20  │ _____ (11) │ DEPT 30  │ _____ (12)
    └──────────┘                └──────────┘
     /    |    \                 /    |    \
┌──────────┐┌──────────┐┌──────────┐  ┌──────────┐┌───────────┐┌───────────┐
│7369 Smith││7566 Gomez││7788 Chung│  │7499 Allen││7564 Martin││7844 Dolske│
└──────────┘└──────────┘└──────────┘  └──────────┘└───────────┘└───────────┘
```

13. In the hierarchical approach, each child will have only one _____ .

14. List two disadvantages of the hierarchical approach.

_____   _____

Network Database

15. In the network approach, we use the terminology of owner records and _____

records.

16. Each member record may have multiple _____ records.

17. In both the network and hierarchical approaches all relationships (parent-child in the hierarchical approach

and owner-member in the network approach) must be defined when you _____

or generate the database.

18. List a disadvantage of the network approach. _____

DATABASE MANAGEMENT SYSTEMS

Label the descriptions below. Choose your answers from the following.

query language   utility   data dictionary   linker   security   hierarchy   database

1. _____ holds the characteristics of the database, items such as field names, field sizes, field descriptions, types of data, and relationships.

2. _____ creates files and dictionaries, monitors performance, copies data, and deletes records.

3. _____ specifies the type of access to each data field in the database for each user.

4. _____ allows the user to retrieve information with user specified criteria as well as output information in a user-specified format.

QUERY LANGUAGES: ACCESS TO THE DATABASE

1. List the three major relational database operations. Choose your answers from the following.

   combine   select   collect   project   join   search   retrieve

   _____

   _____

   _____

2. _____ is the emerging relational database management system query language and is implemented on systems ranging from microcomputers to supercomputers.

DATABASE ADMINISTRATION

1. The _____ coordinates all database activities, which include database design, user coordination, backup and recovery, system security, and performance monitoring.

MANAGING DATA ON A PERSONAL COMPUTER

1. One advantage of a package that supports SQL on the personal computer is that it can directly query _____ databases that also support SQL.

SUMMARY OF DATABASES

1. The database approach represents a better way of _____ data.

2. In the database approach _____ data is minimized since you don't have duplicate fields repeated in single unrelated files.

3. _____ language is used to retrieve data based on user criteria and to output data in a user-specified format.

REVIEW

1. A file is a collection of related _____ .

   a. fields   c. data

   b. information   d. records

2. T   F   A field is also called a data item or data element.

3. A collection of related fields or data elements is called a _____ .

   a. data item   c. record

   b. file   d. database

4. Files are usually stored on a(n) _____ device.

5. Files that are stored on a tape are always organized as _____ files.

6. A major disadvantage of retrieving a record from the middle of a sequential file is that _____ .

   a. space is required for data   c. access speed is slow

   b. key values must be allocated   d. it requires tapes

7. A key is a field or combination of fields that contain data used to _____ records in a sequential file.

   a. unlock   c. organize

   b. lock   d. sequence

8. An index is a list holding the values of a key field and the associated _____ address for each record in the file.

   a. memory   c. disk

   b. tape   d. input

9. T   F   Random retrieval means that any record can be directly retrieved regardless of its position in the file.

10. A relative file contains records that are stored and retrieved according to their

    _____ within the file.

11. The process of using a formula and performing calculations to determine the location of a record is

    called _____ .

    a. indexing   c. hashing

    b. accessing   d. collision

12. When two keys produce the exact same position or address, we have a _____ .

    a. duplicate   c. crash

    b. merger   d. collision

13. Adding records to a file, changing records within the file, and deleting records from the file are all examples

    of _____ .

    a. purging   c. file sustenance

    b. merging   d. updating

14. T F   Data maintenance is another term used in the same manner as file updating.

15. In a database the data is organized in _____ related files.

    a. uniform   c. multiple

    b. direct   d. indexed sequential

16. _____ software allows the user to create, maintain, and extract data and file

    relationships.

    a. Application   c. File management

    b. Operating system   d. Database management

17. _____ software allows the user to create, maintain, and access only a single file

    at a time.

    a. Database management   c. Operating system

    b. File management   d. Application

18. Which of the following is NOT an advantage of database systems over file-oriented systems?

    a. reduced data redundancy   c. reduced data integrity

    b. improved data security   d. integrated files

19. A database in which the data is organized as a collection of tables is called

    a _____ database.

    a. relational   c. network

    b. hierarchical   d. random

20. In a relational database the various tables are related by a common field called

    a(n) _____ .

    a. attribute   c. link

    b. domain   d. key

21. One important advantage of the relational database approach is _____ .

    a. speed   c. data storage savings

    b. flexibility   d. appearance

22. In a _____ database, data is organized in a series like a family tree or

    organization chart.

23. The parent record at the top of a hierarchical database is referred to as

    the _____ .

    a. heir   c. root

    b. father   d. origin

24. Due to the predefined nature of relationships within hierarchical databases, access is

    very _____ .

    a. unreliable   c. fast

    b. slow   d. reliable

25. In a network database, each member can have _____ owners.

    a. exactly one   c. no

    b. multiple   d. infinite

26. T   F   In hierarchical and network databases, data relationships must be defined prior to use within the

    database.

27. A query language is a simple _____ language allowing users to specify the data

    they wish to retrieve.

    a. algebraic   c. programming

    b. Englishlike   d. procedural

28. The select operator is directed to the _____ of a table or relation.

    a. rows   c. domains

    b. columns   d. attributes

29. The project relational operator is directed to the _____ of a relation.

    a. keys   c. domains

    b. rows   d. fields

30. SQL is one of the two most widely used query languages. It is used strictly with

    the _____ database approach.

    a. hierarchical   c. relational

    b. network   d. single file

31. The role of coordinating the use of the database belongs to the _____ .

32. T   F   System security is NOT a responsibility of the database administrator.

33. The first widely used database system for personal computers was _____ .

    a. NOMAD   c. SQL

    b. dBASE   d. AskSam

34. Databases provide a better way of organizing data by relating items in _____ files.

    a. numeric   c. unrelated files

    b. information   d. multiple

Chapter 9

Data Communications

Objectives

1. Define data communications.
2. Describe the basic components of a data communications system.
3. Describe the various transmission media that are used for communication channels.
4. Describe the different types of line configurations.
5. Describe how data is transmitted.
6. Identify and explain the communications equipment that can be used in a data communications system.
7. Describe the functions that communications software can perform.
8. Explain the two major categories of networks and describe the common network configurations.
9. Discuss how personal computers can use data communications.

Chapter Outline

WHAT IS DATA COMMUNICATIONS?

1. Data communications is the _____ from one computer or terminal to another.

2-4. In the illustration below, label the various components. Choose your answers from the following.

computer or terminal   communication equipment

communication network   communication channel

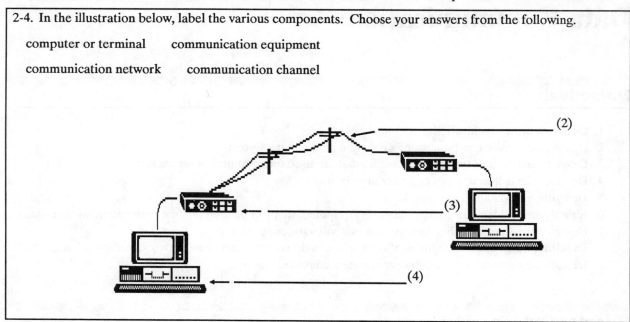

COMMUNICATION CHANNELS

1-3. The illustrations below represent three forms of transmission media.

Label each illustration. Choose your labels from the following.

fiber optics   twisted pair wire   telephone cable   coaxial cable

_____ (1)

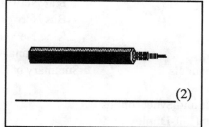

_____ (2)

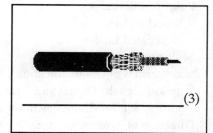

_____ (3)

4. The illustration below is another example of transmission media. The type of transmission media this represents is _____ .

5-7. The illustration below represents an example of data transmission using satellites. Label the illustration.

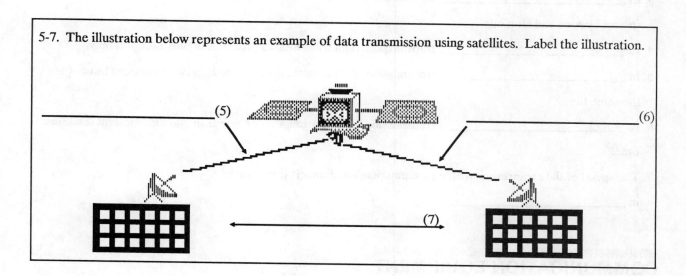

_____ (5)

_____ (6)

_____(7)_____

LINE CONFIGURATIONS

1-2. Label these illustrations of line configurations. Choose your answers from the following.

satellite network   point-to-point   ring   multidrop

_____ (1)

_____ (2)

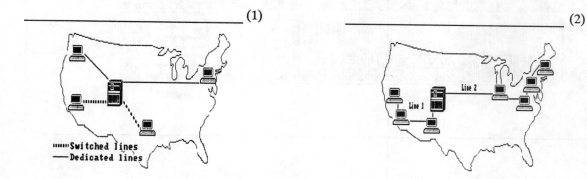

······Switched lines
——Dedicated lines

Line 1   Line 2

CHARACTERISTICS OF COMMUNICATION CHANNELS

Complete these statements about communication channels. Choose your answers from the following.

full-duplex   simplex   synchronous   half-duplex   bits per second

multileaved   asynchronous   bits per second   analog   digital

1. The two types of signals used in communication channels are _____

   and _____ .

2. In _____ transmission, special characters are transmitted in order to coordinate

   the transmission.

3. In _____ transmission, the data that is transmitted is marked in the transmission

   stream by start and stop bits.

4. In _____ transmission, data transmission proceeds in one direction only.

5. In _____ transmission, data transmission proceeds in two directions but not at

   the same time.

6. In _____ transmission, data transmission proceeds in two directions at the same

   time.

7. The speed of data transmission along communication channels is measured

   in _____ .

COMMUNICATION EQUIPMENT

1. The piece of equipment pictured below is an external _____ .

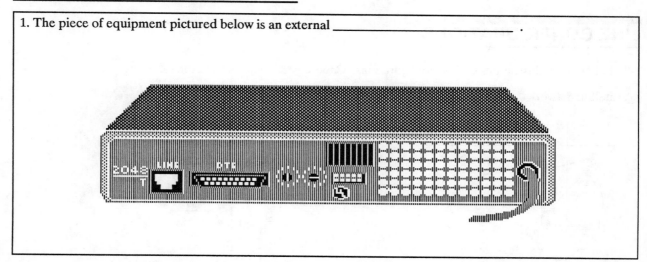

2. The modem pictured below and located within the personal computer is called

a(n) _____ modem.

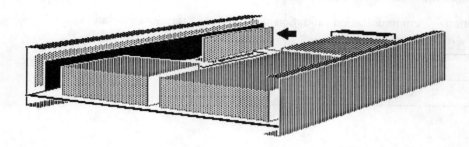

3. The equipment shown below is a(n) _____ .

4. The device illustrated below is routing data to various computing resources and is called

a(n) _____ .

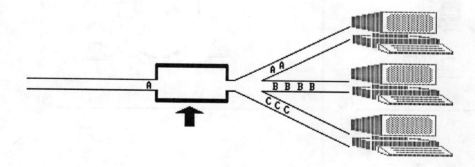

5. _____ is the process of checking connected terminals to see if they have data to

send.

COMMUNICATION SOFTWARE

1. List three major functions of communication software. Choose your answers from the following.

   data encryption   communication validation   dialing   terminal emulation

   _____

   _____

   _____

COMMUNICATION NETWORKS

1. List two major advantages of Local Area Networks (LANs).

   _____   _____

2. WAN is an acronymn for _____ .

NETWORK CONFIGURATIONS

1-3. Label the following network configurations. Choose your answers from the following.

   star network   crisscross network   hierarchical network   ring network   bus network

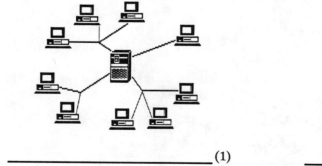

_____ (1)

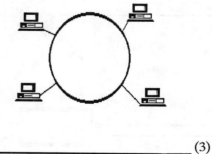

_____ (3)

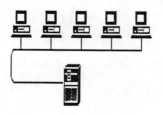

_____ (2)

THE PERSONAL COMPUTER AND DATA COMMUNICATIONS

1. List some ways that the personal computer is used in data communications applications. Choose your answers from the following.

broadband teaching   electronic shopping   satellite video games

commercial databases   home banking   electronic bulletin boards

_____   _____

_____   _____

REVIEW

1. The transmission of data from one computer to another computer over communication channels is called _____ .

   a. networking   c. downloading

   b. data communications   d. data transfer

2. The arrow is pointing to which component of the data communications system?

   a. multidrop line   c. communication channel

   b. communication equipment   d. earth station

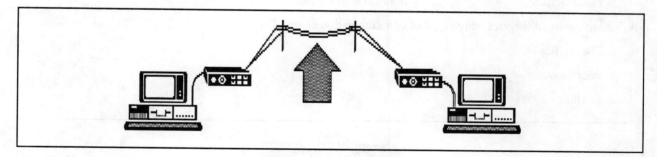

3. The arrow is pointing to which component of the data communications system?

   a. personal computer or terminal   c. communication channel

   b. communication equipment   d. mainframe computer

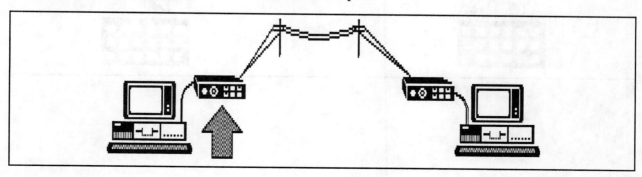

4. The arrow is pointing to which component of the data communications system?

    a. personal computer or terminal   c. communication channel

    b. communication equipment   d. mainframe computer

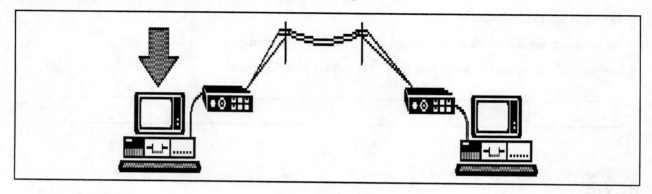

5. T F   Communication channels include various transmission media, including twisted pair wire, coaxial cable, fiber optics, microwaves, and communication satellites.

6. Baseband coaxial cable carries _____ .

    a. one signal at a time   c. multiple signals

    b. radio signals   d. radio waves

7. Broadband coaxial cable carries _____ .

    a. one signal at a time   c. multiple signals

    b. radio signals   d. radio waves

8. The following illustrates which type of communication channel?

    a. fiber optics

    b. microwave

    c. satellite

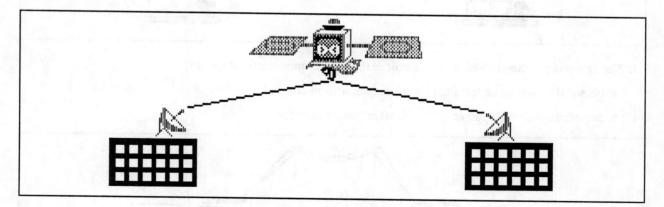

9. _____ are classified as either point-to-point or multidrop.

    a. Receiving locations   c. Line configurations

    b. Host locations   d. Networks

10. T   F   A point-to-point line is a direct line between sending and receiving devices.

11. Multidrop lines commonly use a single line to connect multiple devices such as terminals

    and _____ .

    a. modems   c. fiber optics

    b. telephone wires   d. a host computer

12. _____ signals are used by computer equipment.

    a. Digital   c. Morse code

    b. Analog   d. Microwave

13. _____ signals are used by telephone equipment.

    a. Digital   c. Morse code

    b. Analog   d. Microwave

14. The following illustration represents _____ transmission.

    a. synchronous

    b. asynchronous

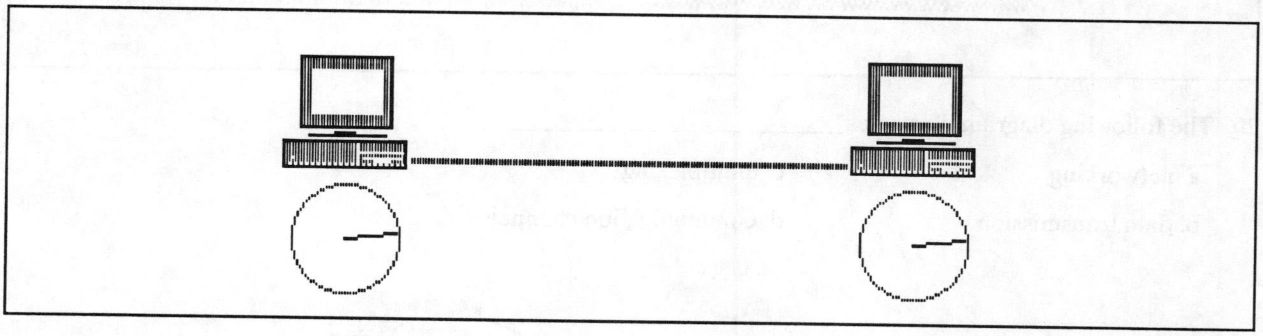

15. The following illustration represents _____ transmission.

    a. synchronous

    b. asynchronous

16. T F In half-duplex transmission, data can be transmitted in both directions along the communications line, but in only one direction at a time.

17. A _____ converts digital signals to analog signals.

    a. multiplexor   c. telephone wire

    b. modem   d. terminal

18. An internal modem is actually a _____ .

    a. box inside the computer   c. circuit board inside the computer

    b. chip inside the computer   d. demodulator

19. The picture below is an example of what type of communication equipment?

    a. a telephone keyboard   c. telephone

    b. an acoustic coupler   d. calculator

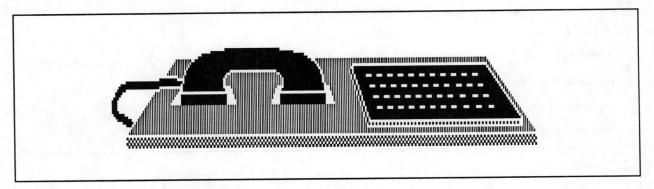

20. The following diagram illustrates _____ .

    a. networking   c. multiplexing

    b. data transmission   d. communication channels

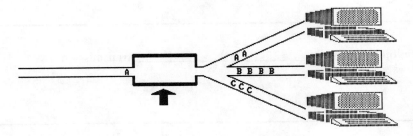

21. A _____ is a collection of terminals, computers, and other equipment that use communication channels to share data.

    a. system   c. network

    b. topology   d. hardware resource sharing

22. The following represents a _____ network.

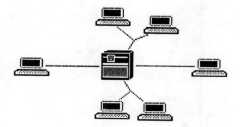

23. For a personal computer to access other computers through data communications, it must have _____ .

a. a modem

c. a phone line

b. communication software

d. all of the above

Chapter 10

Operating Systems and System Software

Objectives

1. Define the terms operating system and system software.
2. Describe the various types of operating systems and explain the differences in their capabilities.
3. Describe the functions of an operating system, including allocating system resources, monitoring system activities, and using utilities.
4. Explain the difference between proprietary and portable operating systems.
5. Name and briefly describe the major operating systems that are being used today.

Chapter Outline

WHAT IS SYSTEM SOFTWARE?

1. List the two categories of software.

_____

_____

2. _____ software controls computer equipment operation.

3. List some examples of system software. Choose your answers from the following.

performs "what if " scenarios   starts up the computer   retrieves information from a database

stores and retrieves files   loads and executes application programs

produces publication-quality materials   performs utility functions

_____   _____

_____   _____

4. _____ software utilizes the computer resources to produce information from data.

5. List some examples of application software. Choose your answers from the following.

spreadsheet   database   operating system   graphics   word processing   disk formatting

_____   _____

_____   _____

WHAT IS AN OPERATING SYSTEM?

1. The operating system is the interface between the end user, the application software, and

computer _____ .

2. The OS supervisor is essential and resides in main memory. List some other names for the OS supervisor. Choose these names from the following.

monitor   kernel   general   executive   master program   control program   loader

_____   _____

_____   _____

_____

3. OS functions other than the OS supervisor are stored on disk and loaded to

_____ when needed.

LOADING AN OPERATING SYSTEM

Complete these steps for "booting" the system.

1. Insert the _____ disk.

2. Turn on the _____ .

3. The _____ execution begins.

The following activities are handled by the operating system after it has been loaded. Complete the statements, choosing your answers from the following.

commands   application   OS   data   execution   allocation

4. loads _____ programs to main memory

5. manages the _____ of application programs

6. processes _____ from the user

TYPES OF OPERATING SYSTEMS

Complete the classification criteria for types of operating systems.

1. number of _____ users

2. number of _____ running

3-6. Label the illustrations of operating systems below. Choose your answers from the following.

multiprogramming   single program   multiprocessing   virtual machine

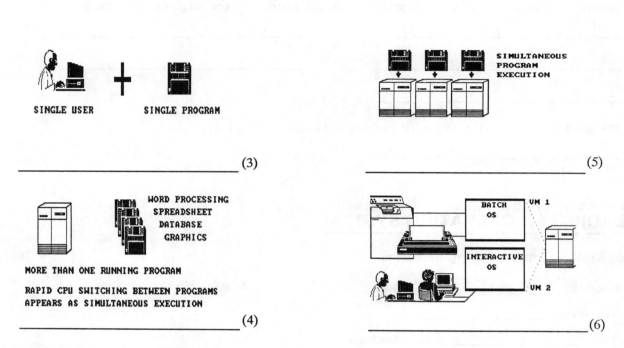

_____ (3)

_____ (4)

_____ (5)

_____ (6)

7-12. Complete the following table.

	SINGLE PROGRAM	MULTI-PROGRAMMING	MULTI-PROCESSING	VIRTUAL MACHINE
NUMBER OF PROGRAMS RUNNING	ONE	(7)	(9)	(11)
NUMBER OF USERS	ONE	(8)	(10)	(12)

FUNCTIONS OF OPERATING SYSTEMS

1-3. In the diagram below, fill in three functions of operating systems. Choose your answers from the following.

maintaining databases   utilities   publishing materials

monitoring activities   allocating system resources

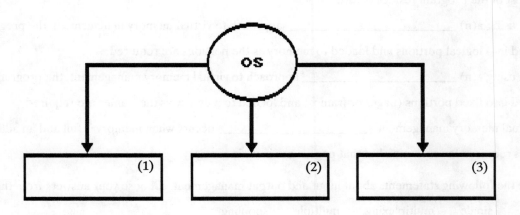

Allocating System Resources

CPU Management

4. With the concept of _____ , the operating system allocates the CPU to various

programs, sharing the CPU resource over time.

5-6. In the two illustrations of time slicing below, label one as time slicing without priority and one as time

slicing with priority.

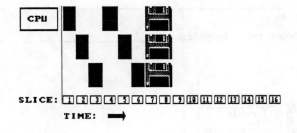

_____ (5)

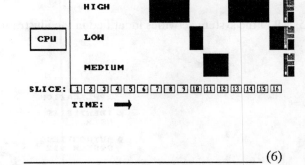

_____ (6)

Complete the following statements about memory management. Choose your answers from the following.

segmentation   paging   inactive   resident   swapping   replacing   active   partitioning

7. The operating system manages memory by _____ the memory into distinct units, each

    capable of holding programs and/or data.

8. In virtual memory situations, only the _____ portion of a program resides in memory.

    The rest of the program resides on disk.

9. When using a(n) _____ approach to virtual memory management, the program is

    divided into logical portions and loaded to memory as the portions are required.

10. When using a(n) _____ approach to virtual memory management, the program is

    divided into fixed portions (pages or frames) and loaded to memory as the frames are required.

11. In virtual memory management, _____ occurs when memory is full and an additional

    page is required for execution but that page is not in main memory.

Complete the following statements about input and output management. Choose your answers from the

following.   single   multiplexing   multiple   spooling

12. Operating systems for mainframe computers typically manage the sharing of disk drives among

    _____ users.

13. _____ is a term used to describe the collection of several print tasks on a disk drive

    with the subsequent printing occurring under control of an operating system program.

Monitoring System Activities

14. List two system performance items that the operating system might monitor. Choose your answers from the

    following.   CPU utilization   password protection   system access   response time

    _____   _____

15. All of the system activities identified in the illustration below relate to system _____ .

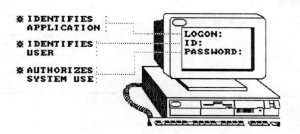

16. The functions of file management, sorting, and editing all fall into the general category of

_____ when associated with the operating system.

POPULAR OPERATING SYSTEMS

Assign the appropriate heading to the list of characteristics below. These characteristics apply to popular operating systems. Choose your answers from the following.

MS-DOS   PC-DOS   TRS-DOS   UNIX   OS/2

portable operating systems   proprietary operating systems

1. _____

    privately owned

    one vendor

2. _____

    licensed by numerous universities

    portable operating system

    extensive library of instructions

    offered by most manufacturers

3. _____

    for IBM PS/2 personal computers

    used with 80286 and 80386 microprocessor chips

    requires 5MB hard disk and 2MB main memory

    runs complex programs

    multiprogramming

    one version has graphics windowing environment

4. _____

    multiple vendors

    retain existing software and data files

5. _____

    Microsoft Disk Operating System

    industry standard for personal computers

    single-user operating system

    IBM version is PC-DOS

REVIEW

1. T   F   A program that tells the computer how to calculate the correct amount to print on a paycheck is an example of system software.

2. The program responsible for formatting disks is classified as _____ software.

    a. systems

    b. applications

3. T F In managing computer resources, the operating system may interface with application software or directly with the end user.

4. T F For a computer to operate, the kernel must be stored in main memory.

5. The routine used to "boot" the operating system is stored in _____ .

    a. primary memory   d. floppy disk

    b. hard disk   e. the application program

    c. ROM

6. T F The operating system prompt indicates to the user that the OS is ready to accept a command.

7. Which type of operating system best supports fault-tolerant computing?

    a. single program   d. multitasking

    b. multiprogramming   e. virtual machine

    c. multiprocessing

8. T F The functions of an operating system include allocating system resources, monitoring system activities, and utilities.

9. T F The system resources that the OS allocates are limited to the CPU, main memory, and output devices.

10. _____ slicing is a common way for an operating system to allocate the CPU resource.

    a. Program   d. Output

    b. Memory   e. Time

    c. Input

11. _____ is the memory allocation technique that the OS uses to transfer fixed size portions of a program between disk and primary memory.

    a. Paging

    b. Segmentation

12. T F The CPU is responsible for managing the input and output processes of the computer.

13. T F Passwords and logon IDs are used by the operating system for monitoring system security.

14. Programs that help manage and sort MS-DOS files are called _____ .

    a. virtual memory management   c. control programs

    b. utilities   d. passwords

15. T   F   Popular operating systems used today include UNIX, MS-DOS, OS/2, and PASCAL.

Chapter 11

Commercial Application Software

WHAT IS COMMERCIAL APPLICATION SOFTWARE?

1. Commercial application software is software that _____ .

2. This software may be designed for the following two types of tasks:

   _____

   _____

GENERAL APPLICATION SOFTWARE

1. General application software provides _____ that allow tasks commonly

   performed in all types of businesses to be done on a computer.

Review of the Four User Tools

2. The four most common tasks for general application software are:

   _____   _____

   _____   _____

3. Three other tasks that commonly employ general application software are:

   _____   _____

   _____

Desktop Publishing

4. _____ enables the user to produce documents that contain both text and

   graphics.

5. What does WYSIWYG stand for in desktop publishing? _____

Electronic Mail

6. Electronic mail allows the user to communicate with other users over _____ .

Project Management

7. Name the five major tasks that can be accomplished with project management software.

_____   _____

_____   _____

_____

FUNCTIONAL APPLICATION SOFTWARE

1. Functional application software is designed to perform a specific _____

or _____ .

Complete the following statements about functional application software. Choose your answers from the

following.   vertical applications   horizontal applications   diagonal applications   lateral applications

2. Functional application software such as an accounting package that is applicable to many different types of

applications or organizations is said to have _____ .

3. Functional application software that has been written specifically for a particular type of business or

organization, such as the construction industry, is said to have _____ .

THE DECISION TO MAKE OR BUY APPLICATION SOFTWARE

1-2. The decision to make or buy application software comes down to a choice between what two types of

software? Fill in the blanks. _____ (1) or _____ (2)

3. Software written for an application that is unique to a specific organization or business is known

as _____ .

HOW TO ACQUIRE COMMERCIAL APPLICATION SOFTWARE

1. List the five steps to follow when acquiring commercial application software.

_____   _____

_____   _____

_____

Evaluating the Application Requirements

2. List the five steps necessary for proper evaluation of application requirements.

_____

_____

_____

_____

_____

Identifying Potential Software Vendors

3. Businesses that specialize in developing software for sale are known

as _____ .

4. Businesses that provide software and equipment for an entire system, and usually provide installation and

training, are known as _____ .

5. A good place to find software suppliers for vertical applications is in _____ .

6. Reviews of individual software packages that are useful in horizontal applications are published regularly

in _____ .

7. Independent specialists who help organizations and businesses identify and implement the right software

solution are known as _____ .

Evaluating Software Alternatives

8. The three key steps when evaluating software alternatives are:

_____

_____

_____

Making the Purchase

9. A _____ provides the user with certain rights and conditions for using software.

Installing the Software

10. Loading the software on the computer system is called _____ .

11. Once the software is loaded, what three steps usually are necessary, particularly for a minicomputer or mainframe computer installation?

_____

_____

_____

REVIEW

1. Software that has already been written and is available for purchase is called _____ .

   a. vendor software
   c. commercial application software
   b. custom software
   d. public domain software

2. The two categories of commercial application software are general application software and _____ application software.

   a. horizontal
   c. business
   b. functional
   d. educational

3. General application software can be used for _____ .

   a. tasks that are commonly performed in all types of businesses

   b. specific tasks or functions

4. T   F   General application software provides a more efficient way to do certain tasks.

5. _____ software allows a user to create professional-looking documents that include both text and graphics.

   a. Spreadsheet
   c. Word processing
   b. Desktop publishing
   d. Graphics

6. T   F   WYSIWYG (What You See Is What You Get) is an important feature of desktop publishing software.

7. T   F   Lotus 1-2-3 is a popular spreadsheet software package.

8. Software that allows users to plan, schedule, track, and analyze the events, resources, and costs of a project is called _____ software.

    a. spreadsheet   c. database task analysis

    b. project management

9. Functional application software can be used for _____ .

    a. tasks that are commonly performed in all types of businesses

    b. specific tasks or functions

10. An accounting software package is an example of _____ application software.

    a. vertical   c. business

    b. horizontal   d. general

11. _____ application software is developed for a unique way of doing business, usually within a specific industry.

    a. Vertical   c. Business

    b. Horizontal   d. General

12. If you needed a program to control the fuel intake rate for the space shuttle, you would most likely decide on which one of the following types of software solutions?

    a. horizontal application   c. custom software

    b. vertical application

13. If you were using a program to manage the inventory of a distribution center for a major shoe manufacturer, you would more than likely be using _____ .

    a. a horizontal application   c. custom software

    b. a vertical application

14. A request for proposal is a written list of an organization's software _____ that is given to prospective software vendors.

    a. inventory   c. compatibility

    b. requirements   d. usage

15. T   F   Identifying potential software vendors can usually be done at a local computer store.

16. T   F   Computer magazines regularly publish reviews of individual (horizontal application) packages and, therefore, are a valuable tool for finding vendors.

17. A benchmark test involves measuring the time it takes to process a set number of transactions and is used to measure the relative _____ of different software packages on the same equipment.

    a. performance   c. ease of use

    b. compatibility   d. capability

18. A _____ is the right to use software under certain terms and conditions.

    a. contract   c. software license

    b. certificate   d. statement of authorization

Chapter 12

The Information System Development Life Cycle

Objectives

1. Describe the six elements of an information system: equipment, software, data, personnel, users, and procedures.
2. Define the term information system and describe the different types of information systems.
3. Explain the five phases of the information system development life cycle: analysis, design, development, implementation, and maintenance.
4. Explain the importance of documentation and project management in the information system development life cycle.
5. Describe how various analysis and design tools, such as data flow diagrams, are used.
6. Explain how program development is part of the information system development life cycle.
7. Explain several methods that can be used for a conversion to a new system.
8. Discuss the maintenance of an information system.

Chapter Outline

WHAT IS AN INFORMATION SYSTEM?

1. An information system is a _____ that provides accurate, timely, and useful information.

2. Name the six elements of an information system.

_____   _____

_____   _____

_____   _____

TYPES OF INFORMATION SYSTEMS

1. List the four broad categories of information systems that use a computer.

_____   _____

_____   _____

WHAT IS THE INFORMATION SYSTEM DEVELOPMENT LIFE CYCLE?

1. Name the five phases of the information system development life cycle.

_____   _____

_____   _____

_____

2. _____ and _____ are two ongoing activities that are performed throughout the information system development life cycle.

PHASE 1--ANALYSIS

1. Define the term "analysis" as it applies to the information system development life cycle.

_____

The Preliminary Investigation

2. What is the most important aspect of the preliminary investigation? _____

Detailed System Analysis

3. A detailed _____ involves a thorough study of the current system but

does not produce solutions to any problems that are identified.

4. Name three key fact-gathering techniques used during detailed system analysis.

_____   _____

_____

5. Describe the three types of information gathered during detailed system analysis.

_____   _____

_____

6. Structured analysis is the use of analysis and _____ such as data flow diagrams,

data dictionaries, structured English, and decision tables and trees.

Making the Decision on How to Proceed

7. A _____ discusses whether a proposed solution is practical and capable

of being accomplished.

8. A _____ identifies the estimated costs of a proposed solution and the

benefits, including potential cost savings, that are expected.

PHASE 2--DESIGN

1. A _____ design is concerned with which programming language will be used in
the development of a system.

2. A _____ design identifies the procedures to be automated and the programming
language, and specifies the equipment needed for the system.

Structured Design Methods

3. _____ focuses on the major functions of the system and breaking them down into
smaller activities.

4. _____ focuses on the data or output of the system and "moves up" to the
processes that are needed to produce the desired output.

Design Activities

5. The illustration below involves the transformation of data from a screen format to a hard-copy format.
That process is called _____ .

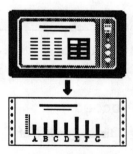

6. Input design, as illustrated below, is concerned with a sequence of inputs and computer responses known as
a _____ .

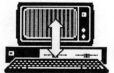

7. During _____ , a systems analyst uses data dictionary information developed

   during the analysis phase and merges it into new or existing system files.

8. During process design, the system analyst specifies exactly what actions will be taken on the

   _____ to create _____ .

9. A system flowchart can be diagrammed with the help of _____ symbols.

   These symbols are shown below.

10. System _____ ensure that only valid data is accepted and processed.

11. List the four basic types of system controls that must be considered by a systems analyst.

   _____   _____

   _____   _____

12. T   F   Test specifications should be developed by an impartial third party, with no assistance from users

    and systems analysts.

test specifications

13. At the end of the design phase, management evaluates the work completed so far by conducting

    a _____ .

14. Building a working model of a new system is known as _____ .

PHASE 3--DEVELOPMENT

1. The two steps of system development are _____

   and _____ .

PHASE 4--IMPLEMENTATION

1. Name three steps in the implementation process.

   _____

   _____

   _____

PHASE 5--MAINTENANCE

1. Define system maintenance.

   _____

2. List the three key elements of system maintenance.

   _____

   _____

   _____

REVIEW

1. An _____ is a collection of elements that provide accurate, timely, and useful

   information.

   a. electronic network   c. operating system

   b. information system   d. information life cycle

2. An information system is comprised of six elements: equipment, _____ , data,

   personnel, users, and procedures.

   a. programmers   c. software

   b. systems analysts   d. documentation

3. A(n) _____ is designed to process data generated by the day-to-day business transactions of a company.

    a. decision support system   c. operational system

    b. management information system d. expert system

4. A(n) _____ is a system designed to help someone reach a decision by summarizing or comparing data from either or both internal and external sources.

    a. decision support system   c. operational system

    b. management information system d. expert system

5. A(n) _____ refers to a computer-based system that generates timely and accurate information for the top, middle, and lower levels of management.

    a. decision support system   c. operational system

    b. management information system d. expert system

6. A(n) _____ combines the knowledge on a given subject of one or more human experts into a computerized system that simulates the human expert's reasoning and decision-making processes.

    a. decision support system   c. operational system

    b. management information system d. expert system

7. T   F   The information systems development life cycle is an organized approach to developing an information system.

8. _____ involves planning, scheduling, reporting, and controlling the individual activities that make up the information systems development life cycle.

    a. Documentation   c. Project management

    b. Analysis   d. Maintenance

9. _____ refers to written materials that are produced throughout the information system development life cycle.

    a. Documentation   c. Gantt chart

    b. Analysis   d. Flowcharting

10. The _____ consists of the separation of a system into its parts to determine how the system works.

    a. analysis phase   d. implementation phase

    b. design phase   e. maintenance phase

    c. development phase

11. A _____ involves both a thorough study of the current system and at least one proposed solution to any problems found.

    a. preliminary investigation   c. logical design

    b. detailed system analysis

12. T   F   A feasibility study and a cost/benefit analysis are performed in the development phase to show whether the proposed system is practical and to show the expected cost and benefits.

13. A physical design is developed in the _____ .

    a. analysis phase   d. implementation phase

    b. design phase   e. maintenance phase

    c. development phase

14. A physical design identifies _____ .

    a. the procedures to be automated

    b. the programming language(s) to be used

    c. the equipment needed for the system

    d. all of the above

15. T   F   There are two major structured design methods: top-down and bottom-up.

16. A way of documenting the process design is with a(n) _____ .

    a. input and output design   c. system flowchart

    b. database design   d. process design

17. A working model of the new system is called a _____ .

18. The _____ consists of the program development and equipment acquisition.

    a. analysis phase   d. implementation phase

    b. design phase   e. maintenance phase

    c. development phase

19. T   F   Writing program specifications, designing the program, coding the program, testing the program, and finalizing the program documentation are included in the implementation phase.

20. The _____ is when people actually begin using the system.

    a. analysis phase   d. implementation phase

    b. design phase   e. maintenance phase

    c. development phase

21. Implementation includes _____ , conversion, and postimplementation evaluation.

    a. performance monitoring   c. training and education

    b. equipment acquisition   d. error correcting

22. T   F   Conversion to the new system is a process of change that can be managed using appropriate methods.

23. The _____ is the process of supporting the information system after it is implemented.

    a. analysis phase   d. implementation phase

    b. design phase   e. maintenance phase

    c. development phase

24. T   F   Maintenance consists of performance monitoring, change management, and error correction.

Chapter 13

Program Development

Objectives

1. Define the term computer program.
2. Describe the five steps in program development: review of program specifications, program design, program coding, program testing, and finalizing program documentation.
3. Explain the concepts of structured program design including modules, control structures, and single entry/single exit.
4. Explain and illustrate the sequence, selection, and iteration control structures used in structured programming.
5. Define the term programming language and discuss the various categories of programming languages.
6. Briefly discuss the programming languages that are commonly used today, including BASIC, COBOL, C, FORTRAN, Pascal, Ada, and RPG.
7. Explain and discuss application generators.
8. Explain the factors that should be considered when choosing a programming language.

Chapter Outline

What Is a Computer Program?
What Is Program Development?
Step 1--Review of Program Specifications
Step 2--Program Design
  Structured Program Design
    Modules
    Control Structures
    Single Entry /Single Exit
  Program Design Tools
    Program Flowcharts
    Pseudocode
    Warnier-Orr
  Structured Walkthroughs
Step 3--Program Coding
Step 4--Program Testing
Step 5--Finalizing Program Documentation
Program Maintenance
Summary of Program Development

What Is a Programming Language?
Categories of Programming Languages
  Machine Language
  Assembly Language
  High-Level Languages
  Fourth-Generation Languages
Programming Languages Used Today
  BASIC
  COBOL
  C
  FORTRAN
  Pascal
  Ada
  RPG
  Other Popular Programming Languages
Application Generators
How to Choose a Programming Language
Summary of Programming Languages

WHAT IS A COMPUTER PROGRAM?

1. List the four items that make up a computer program. Choose your answers from the following.

instructions	language	_____
storage	process	_____
data	input	_____
output	information	_____

WHAT IS PROGRAM DEVELOPMENT?

1-5. List in order the five steps of program development.

_____ (1)   _____ (4)

_____ (2)   _____ (5)

_____ (3)

STEP 1--REVIEW OF PROGRAM SPECIFICATIONS

1. Program specifications usually consist of one or more documents. List six documents.

_____   _____

_____   _____

_____   _____

Complete the statements below about program specifications. Choose the correct answers from the following.

writers   programmer   analyst   users   customer   designer

2. The _____ and _____ , through the system design, have specified *what* is to be done.

3. The _____ determines *how* it is to be done.

STEP 2--PROGRAM DESIGN

1. During program design, a _____ is developed and documented.

2. _____ is a methodology that emphasizes three main program design concepts.

STRUCTURED PROGRAM DESIGN

3. List the three key concepts of structured program design. Choose your answers from the following.

   modules   control structures   _____

   single entry/single exit   multiple subroutines   _____

   structured programming   _____

4. Modules are often referred to as _____ .

5. _____ are often used to decompose and represent the modules of a program.

6. At the conclusion of program decomposition, the entire structure of a program is illustrated by the

   _____ and the relationship of the _____ within the

   program.

7. All logic problems can be solved by three basic control structures:

   _____

   _____

   _____

8. One process occurs immediately after another in the _____ structure.

9. _____ gives programmers a way to represent conditional program logic.

10. _____ means that one or more processes continue to occur so long as a given

    condition remains true.

11. In the _____ structure a condition is tested to determine when the looping will

    terminate.

12. With the _____ control structure, the conditional test is at the end instead of the

    beginning of the loop.

13. _____ means that there is only one entry point and one exit point for each of the

    three control structures.

Program Design Tools

14. List three major design tools. Choose your answers from the following.

flowcharts	Jackson charts	_____
Warnier-Orr	pseudocode	_____
data flow diagrams	data dictionaries	_____

15-22. Label the following flowchart symbols.

_____(15)   _____(16)   _____(17)

_____(18)   _____(19)   _____(20)

_____(21)   _____(22)

23. _____ is a design tool that uses English statements and indentation to show

structure. What is its advantage? _____

24. In the Warnier-Orr approach, the design process focuses on the _____ first.

Structured Walkthroughs

25. During a _____ , the programmer who designs the program explains the

program logic.

26. _____ and programmers also attend walkthroughs after a program has been

designed.

27. The two main purposes of the walkthrough are to _____ and

_____ .

STEP 3--PROGRAM CODING

1. _____ is writing program instructions to process data and produce output.

STEP 4--PROGRAM TESTING

1. Name four types of tests that are performed before "real" data and information from the program can be relied upon.

_____   _____

_____   _____

2-5. Match the definitions below to the following terms:

desk checking _____ (2)   logic testing _____ (4)

syntax error checking _____ (3)   debugging _____ (5)

    a. identifying violations of the program language's grammar rules

    b. locating and correcting program errors during testing

    c. breaking the code into small bits

    d. using test data (expected and unexpected data) to test the program

    e. similar to proofreading a letter

STEP 5--FINALIZING PROGRAM DOCUMENTATION

1. List items that should be included in the program documentation. Choose your answers from the following.

narrative description   comments within program   _____

pseudocode   debugging steps   _____

program flowcharts   program listings   _____

test results   opinions on design   _____

notes on the structured walkthrough   _____

_____

PROGRAM MAINTENANCE

1. Program maintenance is used to correct _____ and make required changes in users' needs.

WHAT IS A PROGRAMMING LANGUAGE?

1. A programming language is a set of words, symbols, and instructions used to _____ with the computer.

CATEGORIES OF PROGRAMMING LANGUAGES

1. What are the four categories of programming languages?

_____   _____

_____   _____

Machine Language

2. _____ is the fundamental language of the processor.

3. Programs written in other categories of languages are eventually _____ to machine language before they are executed.

Assembly Language

4. Assembly language is similar to machine language, but uses abbreviations called _____ or symbolic operation codes.

5. In assembly language, the programmer uses _____ to refer to a memory location rather than its specific numeric locations.

6. _____ generate more than one machine language instruction.

High-Level Languages

7. Circle the statements below that apply to high-level languages.

   a. contain program statements

   b. are usually machine dependent

   c. are usually machine independent

   d. are converted to machine language

       by a compiler or an interpreter

   e. contain program generators

8-9. Fill in the missing labels.

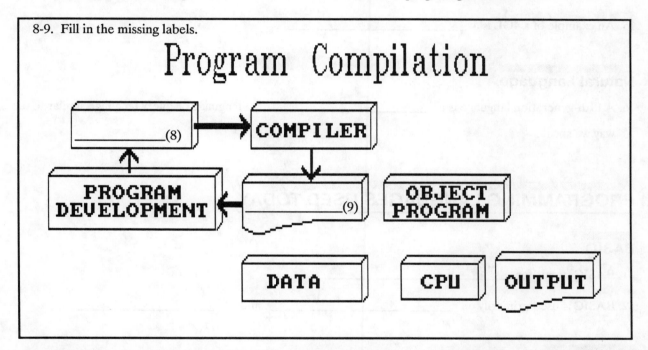

10-12. Fill in the missing labels.

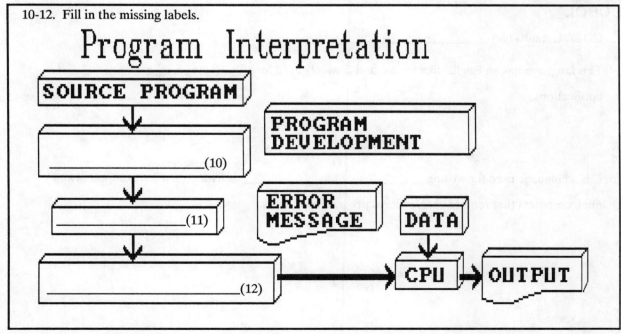

Fourth-Generation Languages

13. Fourth-generation languages (4GLs) are sometimes called _____ and often referred to as _____ .

14. These languages tell the computer _____ to do versus _____ to do it.

15. An example of a 4GL is a _____ .

Natural Language

16. A fifth-generation language is a _____ language or query language similar to the way we speak.

PROGRAMMING LANGUAGES USED TODAY

BASIC

1. BASIC stands for _____ .

2. BASIC is used primarily on _____ and _____ .

COBOL

3. COBOL stands for _____ .

4. This language has an Englishlike format and is widely used for _____ applications.

C

5. C is a language used for writing _____ software on microcomputers and minicomputers that requires professional programming skills.

FORTRAN

6. FORTRAN stands for _____ .

7. Because this language handles _____ easily, it is often used by scientists, engineers, and mathematicians.

Pascal

8. Pascal was named for _____ .

9. Pascal encourages the use of _____ program design.

Ada

10. Ada was named for a mathematician named _____ .

11. Ada facilitates very large _____ and has portability across computers.

RPG

12. RPG stands for _____ .

13. RPG was designed to allow _____ to be generated quickly and easily.

14. What enables this language to be used with a minimum of training? Circle the correct answer.

    a. It uses special forms filled out describing the report.

    b. It uses special formulas to format the reports.

Other Popular Programming Languages

15. _____ is a structured programming language used for scientific and mathematical applications.

16. _____ is a powerful language for manipulating data stored in a table (matrix) format.

17. _____ is similar to C.

18. _____ and _____ are used for artificial intelligence.

19. _____ is used as an educational tool to teach problem-solving skills.

20. _____ is similar to Pascal.

21. _____ is used by educators to write computer-aided instruction programs.

22. _____ combines many of the features of FORTRAN and COBOL.

APPLICATION GENERATORS

1. Another name for application generators is _____ .

2. Application generators produce _____ .

3. A _____ lets the user specify a menu (list) of processing options that can be selected.

4. A _____ allows the user to design an input or output screen by entering the names and descriptions of the input and output data directly on the screen.

HOW TO CHOOSE A PROGRAMMING LANGUAGE

1. Although each programming language has its own unique characteristics, selecting a language for a programming task can be a difficult decision. Circle the factors below that one should consider in making a choice.

a. programming standards

b. portability

c. language suitability

d. maintenance requirements

e. programmer expertise

f. user friendliness

g. language availability

h. interfacing needs

REVIEW

1. A computer program is a set of instructions that _____ .

   a. processes data into information

   b. are usually written by a programmer

   c. are usually written in one of many languages

   d. all of the above

2. The first step in program development is _____ .

   a. review of program specifications   c. program design

   b. program coding   d. initiating program documentation

3. In structured program design, programs are separated into _____ .

   a. subsets   c. nodes

   b. modules   d. pages

4. The control structure used to repeat a process is called _____ .

   a. sequence   c. selection

   b. iteration   d. what-if

5. Looping is accomplished in two forms, DO WHILE and DO _____ .

   a. GO TO   c. UNTIL

   b. LOOP   d. AS

6. In structured program design, control structures should have _____ .

   a. a single condition   c. fewer than two GO TOs

   b. no more than 10 statements   d. a single entry/exit

7. Once a program is coded, the next step is _____ .

8. Program logic testing is accomplished by _____ .

   a. using expected data   c. using unexpected data

   b. desk and syntax checking   d. all of the above

9. In program development, documenting a program is _____ .

   a. the final step   c. the first step

   b. an ongoing process   d. none of the above

10. High-level languages are designed with the _____ in mind.

11. T   F   Machine language is the language to which all other languages are converted.

12. T F Assembly language is a high-level language because it is closely related to the design of the computer.

13. The function of a compiler is to _____ high-level languages.

14. The definition of a fourth-generation language is that it is nonprocedural, user-friendly, and deals with _____ .

   a. what versus how   b. how versus what

15. The first programming language to encourage structured program design was _____ .

16. Two common business-oriented languages are _____ .

   a. C and FORTRAN   c BASIC and Pascal

   b. COBOL and RPG   d. Ada and BASIC

17. Programs designed to shorten program development time include program, menu, and screen _____ .

18. T F A factor to consider when choosing a language is future maintenance.

Chapter 14

Career Opportunities in the Age of Information Processing

Objectives

1. Discuss the three areas that provide the majority of computer-related jobs.
2. Describe the career positions available in an information systems department.
3. Describe information processing career opportunities in sales, service and repair, consulting, and education and training.
4. Discuss the compensation and growth trends for information processing careers.
5. Discuss the three fields in the information processing industry.
6. Discuss career development, including professional organizations, certification, and professional growth and continuing education.

Chapter Outline

The Information Processing Industry
  The Computer Equipment Industry
  The Computer Software Industry
  Information Processing Professionals
What Are the Career Opportunities in
  Information Processing?
  Working in an Information Systems Department
  Sales
  Service and Repair
  Consulting
  Education and Training
Compensation and Growth Trends for
  Information Processing Careers

Preparing for a Career in Information Processing
  What Are the Fields in the Information
    Processing Industry?
  Obtaining Education for Information Processing
    Careers
Career Development in the Information Processing
  Industry
  Professional Organizations
  Certification
  Professional Growth and Continuing Education
Summary of Computer Career Opportunities

THE INFORMATION PROCESSING INDUSTRY

1. Name the three areas where job opportunities in the information processing industry are found.

   _____   _____

   _____

WHAT ARE THE CAREER OPPORTUNITIES IN INFORMATION PROCESSING?

1. Using the list below, name the five categories of jobs in an information systems department.

   operations   programming   _____

   data administration   hardware administration _____

   information center   system analysis and design _____

   software library administration   _____

                                                       _____

2. _____ personnel are responsible for carrying out tasks such as operating the computer equipment located in the data center, providing telecommunications, control and scheduling services, data entry, and maintaining the tape and/or disk library.

3. Name the two major roles of the data administration section of the information processing department.

   _____   _____

4. What two roles do systems analysis and design personnel fulfill?

   _____   _____

5. Programming personnel include application programmers and _____ programmers.

6. The role of information center personnel is to provide _____

   and _____ .

7. _____ representatives in the information processing industry must have strong interpersonal, or "people," skills, but a general knowledge of computers and a specific understanding of the product they are selling are not necessary.

8. Someone who draws upon his or her computer experience to give advice to others is known as

a _____ .

9. T   F   The high demand by private industry for teachers with computer education and training experience

has helped create a high demand at colleges and universities for qualified instructors with the same skills.

COMPENSATION AND GROWTH TRENDS FOR INFORMATION PROCESSING CAREERS

1. Name the industry in which information processing professionals are likely to receive the highest pay.

_____

2. Fill in the following salary table for programming personnel.

PROGRAMMING	
Commercial	_____
Engineering/Scientific	_____
Microcomputer	_____
Minicomputer	_____
Software Engineer	_____
Systems Software	_____
(less than 2 years of experience)	

PREPARING FOR A CAREER IN INFORMATION PROCESSING

1. Name the three major fields in the information processing industry.

_____   _____

_____

2. List two career opportunities in computer engineering.

_____   _____

3. Six career opportunities are available in computer information systems. List them below.

_____   _____

_____   _____

_____   _____

4. List three career opportunities in computer science.

_____   _____

_____

5. Educational institutions and _____ are two sources of information and training in computers.

CAREER DEVELOPMENT IN THE INFORMATION PROCESSING INDUSTRY

1. One way to further your professional growth and continue your education in computers is to join one or more _____ organizations, such as the Association for Computing Machinery (ACM) or the Data Processing Management Association (DPMA).

2. _____ programs are a way to encourage and recognize the efforts of professionals who improve their level of knowledge about their professions.

REVIEW

1. As society becomes more information oriented, _____ are becoming an integral part of most jobs.

2. Computers, tape drives, terminals, and printers are manufactured by companies in the _____ industry.

   a. informations   c. computer software

   b. data processing   d. computer equipment

3. _____ is a leading manufacturer of mini- and mainframe computers.

   a. Ashton-Tate   c. Intel

   b. IBM   d. AT&T

4. Leaders in the computer software industry include _____ .

   a. Lotus   c. Ashton-Tate

   b. Microsoft   d. all of the above

5. In an information systems department, program development would be done by a _____ .

    a. database administrator   c. systems analyst

    b. programmer   d. computer operator

6. T   F   The primary responsibility of data administration is the maintenance and control of an organization's database.

7. An information center provides _____ services within an organization to help users meet their departmental and individual processing needs.

    a. computer   c. library and information

    b. teaching and consulting   d. software and hardware

8. _____ are often the most highly compensated employees in a computer company.

    a. Programmers   c. Sales representatives

    b. Systems analysts   d. Consultants

9. T   F   Service and repair technicians troubleshoot, solve problems, and have a strong background in electronics.

10. _____ draw upon their experience and expertise to give advice to others for tasks such as system selection, system design, and communication network design and installation.

    a. Consultants   c. Managers

    b. Trainers   d. System design specialists

11. Compensation is a function of experience and _____ .

    a. knowledge   c. demand

    b. personality   d. work ethics

12. Research shows that the fastest-growing computer career positions between 1982 and 1995 will be _____ .

    a. systems analysts   d. computer repair technicians

    b. machine operators   e. all of the above

    c. applications programmers

13. Computer Information Systems (CIS) refers to the use of computers in areas relating to _____ .

    a. communications   c. business

    b. information processing   d. financial management

14. _____ includes the technical aspects of computers, such as hardware operation and systems software.

    a. Computer science   c. Computer information systems

    b. Computer engineering

15. _____ deals with the design and manufacturing of electronic computer components and hardware.

    a. Computer science   c. Computer information systems

    b. Computer engineering

16. T   F   Computer development involves developing skills and increasing recognition among peers.

17. _____ have been formed by people who have common interests and a desire to share their knowledge.

    a. Computer cooperatives   c. Sharewares

    b. Professional organizations   d. Comdex

18. T   F   The Certificate of Data Processing (CDP) is the best known certification program in the information processing industry.

19. T   F   Computer professionals can stay current by participating in professional growth and continuing education activities such as conferences, workshops, conventions, and trade shows.

Chapter 15

Trends and Issues in the Information Age

Objectives

1. Discuss the electronic devices and applications that are part of the automated office.
2. Describe the technologies that are developing for the automated factory, including CAD, CAE, CAM, and CIM.
3. Discuss the use of personal computers in the home.
4. Explain guidelines for purchasing personal computers.
5. Discuss social issues related to computers, such as computer crime and privacy.

Chapter Outline

INFORMATION SYSTEMS IN BUSINESS

The Automated Office

1-7. New devices and services provide increased productivity in the automated office, sometimes known as the electronic office. Using the list below, match the devices and services that are likely to be found in modern automated offices.

teleconferencing   word processing   electronic mail   facsimile   image processing   voice mail

desktop publishing   teletype   dictaphone   manual typewriter   copy machine

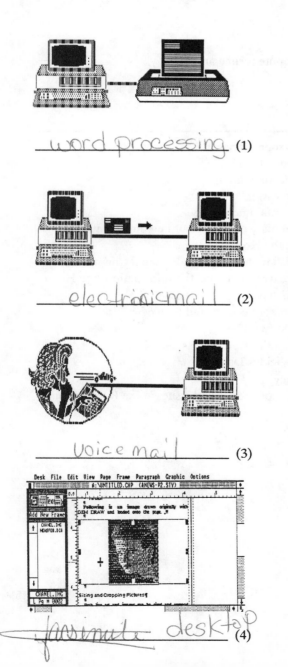

word processing (1)

electronicmail (2)

voice mail (3)

facsimile desktop (4)

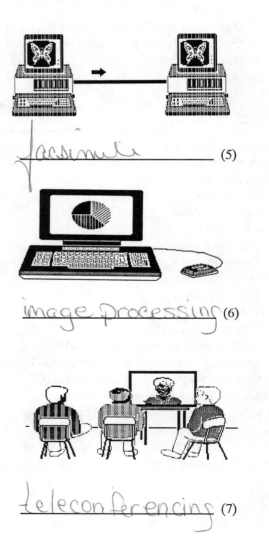

facsimile (5)

image processing (6)

teleconferencing (7)

The Automated Factory

8. CAD is the acronym for _computer aided design_

9. _CAE_____ is the use of computers to test product designs.

10. Computer-aided manufacturing (CAM) is the use of computers to control production equipment in an

   automated _factory_____ .

11-14. The concept of computer-integrated manufacturing (CIM) is to integrate all phases of the

   manufacturing process. Fill in the blocks on the diagram below. Choose your answers from the following.

   production planning   package designing   product design

   computer automation   product distribution   manufacturing

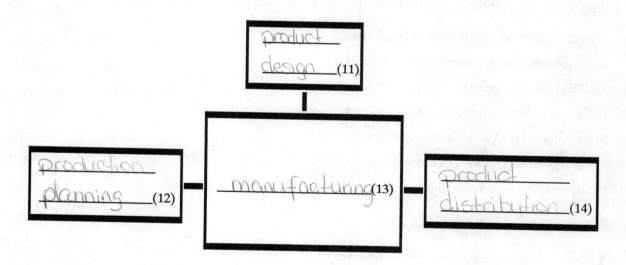

product design (11)

production planning (12)

manufacturing (13)

product distribution (14)

COMPUTER – INTEGRATED MANUFACTURING

BRINGING THE INFORMATION AGE HOME

1. The concept of bringing the information age home refers to the use of _____

   computers in the home.

2. List five common uses for personal computers located in the home. Choose the major uses from the following.

personal services   education   *personal services*

telecommuting   control of home systems   *telecommuting*

entertainment   monitoring cooking devices *entertainment*

education

control of home devices

3. _____*CAI*_____ teaches through drills and practices as well as through simulation.

Guidelines for Buying a Personal Computer

4. List six guidelines for buying a personal computer. Choose from the list of options below.

Select the suppliers for software and equipment.

Learn the memory-chip manufacturing process.

Become computer literate.

Define and prioritize the tasks you want to perform on your computer.

Select software packages that best meet your needs.

Select equipment that will run software you have selected.

Purchase software and equipment.

Step 1: _____

Step 2: _____

Step 3: _____

Step 4: _____

Step 5: _____

Step 6: _____

Social Issues

1. Name the four major social issues that computer users must face.

_____   _____

_____   _____

Review

1. Automated offices use electronic devices such as computers, facsimile machines, and computerized telephone systems to improve _____ .

   a. revenues   c. productivity

   b. relationships   d. data security

2. Electronically creating, storing, revising, and printing documents is called _____ .

   a. database management   c. facsimile

   b. word processing   d. desktop publishing

3. _____ is the ability to transmit messages to and receive messages from other computers.

   a. Electronic mail   c. Facsimile

   b. Word processing   d. Desktop publishing

4. T F The automated factory uses computer-controlled equipment to increase productivity.

5. _____ uses a computer and special graphics software to aid in product design.

   a. CAE   c. CAM

   b. CAD

6. _____ is the use of computers to control production equipment.

   a. CAE   c. CAM

   b. CAD

7. _____ is the use of computers to test product designs.

   a. CAE   c. CAM

   b. CAD

8. T F CIM is the total integration of the manufacturing process using computers.

9. T F Personal computers in the home are used for business tasks as well as for personal services.

10. T   F   Computers are used in some homes to control the timing for lighting and landscape sprinkler systems.

11. Individuals who work at home and communicate with their offices by using personal computers and communication lines are _____ .

    a. telecommuting   c. probably using a modem

    b. cheating   d. highly compensated professionals

12. CAI software is used for _____ in the home.

    a. entertainment   c. budgeting

    b. education

13. T   F   Being computer literate is not a great advantage when considering purchasing a computer for the home.

14. T   F   You should be certain that your hardware and software choices are compatible before purchasing them.

15. The term "computer _____ " refers to the safeguards established to prevent and detect unauthorized use and deliberate or accidental damage to computer systems and data.

    a. passwords   c. security

    b. regulation   d. accident prevention

16. T   F   A very dangerous type of malicious damage is done by a virus, a program designed to copy itself into other software and spread through multiple systems.

Introduction to DOS

Objectives

1. "Boot" your microcomputer.
2. Enter the time and date, if required.
3. Establish the system default disk drive.
4. List a disk directory.
5. Cancel commands.
6. Format diskettes, using /S and /V.
7. Use file specifications to address files on various disks.
8. Copy files on the same disk and from one disk to another.
9. Rename and erase files.
10. Organize and manage file subdirectories on a hard disk.
11. Start application programs.

Chapter Outline

Introduction
    Operating Systems for IBM PCs
    DOS Versions
Using the Disk Operating System (DOS)
    Starting the Computer
    Setting the Date and Time
    The DOS Prompt
    The Default Drive
Entering Disk Operating System (DOS)
    Commands
    Internal and External Commands
Directory Command (DIR)
    Displaying Directories of Other Disks
    Pausing Directory Listings
    Canceling a Command (Break)
Formatting a Diskette
    The FORMAT Command
    Formatting a System Disk (/S Option)
    Assigning a Volume Label (/V Option)
CLS Command
Managing Data and Program Files on Disks
    Assigning File Specifications

Copy Command
Using the Copy Command
    Copying Files From One Diskette to Another
    Copying to the Default Disk
    Copying a File to the Same Diskette
    Global Filename Characters ("Wildcards")
    Using Wildcards with DOS Commands
RENAME Command
ERASE and DEL Commands
    Removing Files
Using Directories and Subdirectories
    Directory Entries and Subdirectories
    The PROMPT Command
    Making Subdirectories
    Changing Directories
    Specifying a Path to Subdirectories and Files
    Managing Files Within Subdirectories
    Removing Subdirectories
Loading a Program
Summary

INTRODUCTION

1. A(n) _____ is one or more programs that control and manage the operation of the computer.

2. DOS is an acronym for _____ .

In items 3-4, place the appropriate operating system next to the descriptions. Choose your answers from the following.   MS-DOS   UNIX   PC-DOS

3. _____ distributed by IBM for its line of personal computers

4. _____ distributed by Microsoft for all IBM-compatibles

5. Variations of an operating system are called _____ .

USING THE DISK OPERATING SYSTEM (DOS)

1. To start a floppy-based microcomputer, you would place the _____ diskette in the appropriate floppy disk drive and turn the power on.

2. The process described in item 1 above is called "_____" your computer.

3. To boot a _____ disk system you would merely turn the power on.

4. If you wish to restart or reboot your system, you could go through the method described in items 1 and 3 above, or you could use a key sequence. List the key sequence required to restart your computer.

   Choose your key sequence from the following.   Ctrl Esc   Ctrl Alt Del   Esc Esc Esc

   _____   Ctrl Alt End   Home   Ctrl Alt

5. One of the first tasks required by DOS is to set the _____

   and _____ .

6. If you are using a typical floppy-based system, DOS will print an A > on your screen. This is called the

   DOS _____ .

7. The A of the A > is an indication that drive A on your floppy-based system is

   the _____ drive.

8. List the command required to change the default drive from the A drive to the B drive. Choose your answer from the following.   b   Set to B   Change to B   B:

_____

9. DOS commands are executed by pressing the _____ key.

10. What is the usual name for the disk drive associated with a fixed disk? _____

ENTERING DISK OPERATING SYSTEM (DOS) COMMANDS

1. Internal commands are part of the operating system and are always available to the user. List three internal operating system commands. Choose your answers from the following.

COPY   DIR   CHKDSK   _____

DISKCOPY   ERASE   RENAME   _____

DEL   CLS   FORMAT   _____

2. _____ commands are DOS commands that are stored on the DOS diskette and must be read into main memory before they can be executed.

DIRECTORY COMMAND (DIR)

Complete the following statements about the directory command. Choose your answers from the following.

DIR /W   Ctrl Alt Del   DIR B: Ctrl Break   DIR   DIR B   DIR /P   Escape

1. To obtain a directory of the default drive you would issue the command _____ .

2. If you wanted a directory of drive B (not the current default drive), you would issue the command _____ .

3. To interrupt a directory listing, you would press the key sequence _____, then press any key to continue.

4. The command _____ automatically pauses a directory listing when the screen is full.

5. You can utilize the total width of the screen for your directory listing by using the command _____ .

FORMATTING A DISKETTE

Complete the following statements about the format command. Choose your answers from the following.

FORMAT \v   FORMAT b: FORMAT /S

FORMAT /V   FORMAT \SYSTEM   FORMAT A:

1. If drive A is the default drive and you wanted to format a disk in drive B, you would use the

    command _____ .

2. In order to format a diskette and place DOS on that disk, you would use the

    command _____ .

3. If you wished to assign a volume label to a disk during the formatting process, you would use the

    command _____ .

CLS COMMAND

1. The abbreviation CLS stands for _____ .

MANAGING DATA AND PROGRAM FILES ON DISKS

1. A _____ file is a collection of data created by application or system programs and

    used by the programs.

2. A _____ file contains machine-readable instructions that the computer follows to

    perform its tasks.

Use the following file specification for items 3-6.

    C:\WP\FILES\TEST1.DOC

3. The C in the file specification is the _____ drive letter, and it is always followed by

    a colon.

4. The \WP\FILES\ portion of the file specification is the _____ . It identifies the

    specific subdirectory of interest.

5. The TEST1 part of the file specification is the _____ .

6. The .DOC part of the file specification is the optional _____ . It is used to further

    identify the file.

7. Filenames with extensions of . _____ and . _____ are executable programs.

8. _____ files, which have the extension of .BAT, contain a series of DOS commands to be executed in sequence.

COPY COMMAND

1. Consider the following illustration. If the default drive is A, what command would you issue to accomplish the task of copying the file DOSQUIZ.DOC to drive B?

_____

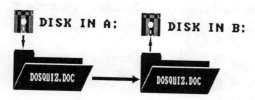

2. Consider the illustration below. The disk in drive B has received all of the files from the disk in drive A. The disk in drive B is said to be a _____ of the disk in drive A.

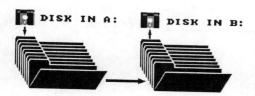

3-4. Fill in the blanks in the illustration below. Choose your answers from the following.

target   terminator   source   command_   receptor   original

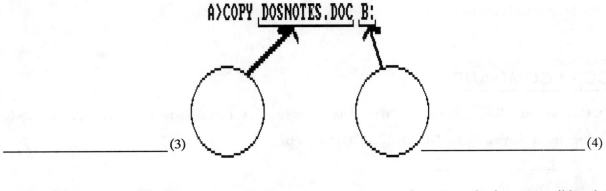

_____ (3)

_____ (4)

5. To copy more than one file you can use _____ characters, also known as wildcards.

6. When the _____ character is used as part of a filename or extension, it is said to be a wildcard.

7. Issue a command using the * wildcard approach to copy all files from the current drive to drive B. Choose your command from the following.   COPY A:dos.* B: COPY   A:ALL b:

   COPY   *.*   B: COPY   A   B:

   _____

8. What command copies all files with a .COM extension from the A drive to the B drive?

   _____

9. What command copies all files beginning with the letter "G" from the A drive to the B drive?

   _____

10. The ? character is a single character _____ , whereas the * is a multiple character wildcard.

11. Issue a command to copy all files with an extension of .BA followed by any other character to the disk in the B drive. Use the ? wildcard in this command. Assume A: is the default drive.

    _____

12-18. Match the following commands with the appropriate description.

a. A:>DIR   B:*.EXE

b. C:>DIR   \WP\FILES*.DOC

c. A:>COPY   *.BAT   C:\BATCH

d. A:>COPY   C:\BATCH*.*   B:

e. C:\UTILITY>COPY   *.EXE   A:

f. C:\BASIC>COPY   *.BAS   A:

g. C:\WORK>COPY   *.*   \BACKUP

h. C:>DIR\FILES\WP*.DOC

i. UTILITY>COPY *.A

j. CBASIC\COPY BAS* A:

12. Copy all files from the subdirectory BATCH on the C drive to the B drive.

_____

13. Produce a directory of all files on the B drive which have an extension of .EXE.

_____

14. Copy all files from the subdirectory WORK on the C drive to the subdirectory BACKUP on the C drive.

_____

15. Produce a directory of the subdirectory FILES within the subdirectory WP. List only those files with an extension of .DOC.

_____

16. Copy all files with an extension of .EXE from the C drive within the subdirectory UTILITY to the A drive.

_____

17. Copy all files with an extension of .BAS from the C drive within the subdirectory BASIC to the A drive.

_____

18. Copy all files from the A drive with an extension of .BAT to the subdirectory BATCH on the C drive.

_____

RENAME COMMAND

1. The rename command is designed to change the _____ of a file.

2. To change the name of the file NOTECOPY to DOSFILE you would issue the

   command _____ .

3. To rename all files with an extension of .BAK to files with an extension of .BAC using a wildcard, what

   command would you use? _____

ERASE AND DEL COMMANDS

1. The ERASE and DEL commands are identical commands designed to _____ a file

from a directory or subdirectory. (Fill in the above blank without using the words erase or delete.)

USING DIRECTORIES AND SUBDIRECTORIES

1. The disk's main directory is automatically named by DOS and is named \. It is called the

directory.

2. All directories under the root directory are called subdirectories, and the user must name these. In the

diagram below, circle the name of each subdirectory under the root directory.

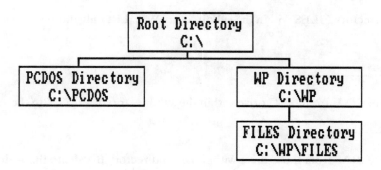

3. To create a new subdirectory you would use the command _____ .

4. You would use the command _____ directory to move to another directory.

5. When you change from one directory to another directory, the directory to which you changed becomes

the _____ directory.

6. To remove a directory, DOS requires that the directory has no _____ in it and has

no subdirectories under it.

7. The command for removing a directory is _____ .

LOADING A PROGRAM

1. To load a program and initiate its execution under DOS, you enter the _____ of the
program.

REVIEW

1. The process of reading an operating system into main memory is called _____ .
   - a. executing
   - b. booting
   - c. entering
   - d. startup
   - e. formatting

2. T   F   Booting a hard disk system can be done with the drive A empty.

3. To restart (reboot) the system you would press the Ctrl, _____ , and Del keys.
   - a. Break
   - b. Shift
   - c. Alt
   - d. Home

4. To list the files in C:\WP\FILES you would type _____ .
   - a. C:DIR   \WP\FILES
   - b. C:LIST   \WWWWP\FILES
   - c. A:DIR   C:\WP\FILES
   - d. a or c, depending on the default drive

5. T   F   A   /p is optional with the DIR command if you want to pause the listing with each full screen.

6. T   F   DIR   /W displays a list of files in a wide format.

7. To cancel a command press _____ .
   - a. Ctrl - End
   - b. Ctrl - Del
   - c. Ctrl - C
   - d. Ctrl - Break
   - e. Break
   - f. c or d
   - g. b or e

8. The _____ command establishes sectors on a diskette and performs other
functions that allow the diskette to store files.
   - a. CHKDSK
   - b. DIR
   - c. FORMAT
   - d. AUTOEXEC

9. When you type A: _____ , this is one of the messages you will see:

Volume label (11 characters, ENTER for none)?

a. DIR   B: c. CHKDSK   B:

b. FORMAT   B:/S   d. FORMAT   B:/V

10. T   F   The CLS command creates large sectors on your diskette.

11. DOS identifies the files on a disk by a combination of which of the following specifications?

a. FILENAME, TIME, DATE

b. DRIVE\PATH\FILENAME.EXTENSION

c. FILENAME, MEMORY ALLOCATION

d. none of the above

12. T   F   A DOS batch file contains a series of DOS commands to be executed in sequence.

13. A common use of the COPY command is to make working copies of program and data disks, producing _____ .

a. new files

b. file disks

c. backup copies

14. On a hard disk system, the COPY command can transfer a duplicate file from one

_____ to another.

a. diskette   c. subdirectory

b. directory   d. all of the above

15. The _____ file is the file to be copied.

a. source   c. program

b. DOS   d. original

16. The COPY command can make a copy (WITH A DIFFERENT FILENAME) by including the name of the _____ file (for example: A:COPY   AUTOEXEC.BAT AUTOEXEC.BAK).

a. new   c. second

b. target   d. backup

17. To change the name of a file from TEST1.DOC to QUIZ2.DOC, enter _____ .

    a. NAME1.DOC   QUIZ2.DOC

    b. CHANGE   TEST1.DOC   TO   QUIZ2.DOC

    c. RENAME   TEST1.DOC   QUIZ2.DOC

    d. COPY   TEST1.DOC   TO   QUIZ2.DOC

18. To remove a file named TEST1.DOC from a disk, type _____ .

    a. DELETE   TEST1.DOC   c. ERASE   TEST1.DOC

    b. REMOVE   TEST1.DOC   d. either a or c

19. A disk's main directory is called the _____ directory.

    a. main   c. root

    b. original   d. standard

20. Filenames on disks can be grouped into _____ .

    a. index lists   c. directories and subdirectories

    b. sector allocations   d. bytes

21. The MKDIR or MD command will _____ .

    a. manage directory files   c. create a file copy

    b. make a directory on a disk   d. either a or b

22. To change from the root directory to a directory of data files under a spreadsheet directory named 123, type _____ .

    a. CH/DATA   c. CD   \123\DATA

    b. GOTO 123 DATA   d. C:\123\DATA

23. T F   To remove a directory from the disk, you must first remove all files from the directory.

24. The RMDIR or RD command will _____ .

    a. rename a directory   c. rename all files in a directory

    b. remove a directory   d. remove all files in a directory

ANSWERS

Chapter 1: An Introduction to Computers

What Is a Computer? (1.2)
1. data

What Does a Computer Do? (1.2)
1. input, process, output, storage
2. information processing cycle
3. words, numbers, pictures
4. letters, forecasts, presentations
5. Information processing, electronic data processing
6. storage
7. storage
8. output
9. processor
10. input

Why Is a Computer So Powerful? (1.3)
1. input, process, output, storage
2. quickly, accurately, reliably

How Does a Computer Know What to Do? (1.3)
1. instructions
2. computer program, program instructions software

Information Processing: A Business Application (1.3)
1. Data
2. Information

The Information Processing Cycle (1.4)
1. Input
2. Process
3. Output
4. Storage

What Are the Components of a Computer? (1.4)
1. input devices, processor unit, output device, auxiliary storage

2. keyboard, floppy disk, fixed disk
3. addition, subtraction, multiplication, division
4. $A > B$, $A = B$, $A < B$
5. data, program instructions
6. central processing unit, CPU
7. printer, computer screen
8. instructions, data
9. peripheral devices

Categories of Computers (1.6)
1. microcomputer, minicomputer, mainframe computer, supercomputer
2. speed, price, size, processing capabilities
3. less than $10,000, approximately $25,000 to several hundred thousand dollars, several hundred thousand dollars up to several million dollars, millions of dollars

Computer Software (1.6)
1. word processing, spreadsheet, graphics, database
2. Load
3. data
4. process
5. Output
6. Save

What Are the Elements of an Information System? (1.7)
1. equipment, software, data, personnel, users, procedures

A Tour of an Information Systems Department (1.7)
1. multiuser computer
2. information systems, data processing, computer
3. terminal, fixed disk, keyboard
4. processor
5. printer, fixed disk, monitor
6. magnetic disk, magnetic tape
7. removable, fixed
8. tape library
9. disks, tapes
10. main memory
11. source documents

12. data entry, computer operator, systems analyst, computer programmer, database administrator
13. Information Systems Department Manager
14. Systems Manager
15. Programming Manager
16. Operations Manager
17. initiate requests, interact with systems analyst, continuing requests
18. Procedures

The Evolution of the Computer Industry (1.9)

1. UNIVAC I
2. IBM
3. Dr. Hopper
4. FORTRAN
5. Transistors
6. IBM 360
7. Dr. Kemeny: BASIC
8. DEC Minicomputer
9. IBM: Software unbundled
10. Dr. Hoff: Microprocessor
11. Jobs & Wozniak: Apple
12. VisiCalc
13. Microsoft: MS-DOS
14. IBM PC
15. Kapor: Lotus 1-2-3
16. Intel 80386
17. IBM: Application System 400

Review (1.9)

1. data
2. storage
3. Information
4. T
5. T
6. F
7. computer programs
8. information
9. T
10. input device
11. processor
12. main memory

13. output device
14. T
15. supercomputers
16. T
17. microcomputers
18. T
19. application software
20. six
21. Users
22. systems analyst
23. database administrator

Chapter 2: Microcomputer Applications:
User Tools

An Introduction to General
Microcomputer Applications (2.2)

1. microcomputer
2. broad
3. user friendly
4. function keys, menus, screen prompts, icons
5. icons
6. function keys
7. screen prompts

The Four Most Common
General Appllcations (2.3)

1. word processing, electronic spreadsheet, database, graphicx

Word Processing Software:
A Document Productivity Tool (2.3)

1. online spell checking, online thesaurus, merge/retyping capability, faster, more accurate
2. Online spell checking, merge/retyping capability, online thesaurus
3. delete, insert, replace
4. copy
5. move
6. boldfacing, underlining, changing fonts
7. formatting
8. Spelling checkers
9. Thesaurus software
10. Grammar checkers

11. change margins, change page size, change print style
12. reprint
13. file
14. transmitting
15. insert/move
16. delete features
17. screen control
18. printing

Electronic Spreadsheet Software: A Number Productivity Tool (2.5)

1. faster, more accurate, easier to use, more efficient
2. Rows, columns, cells
3. row
4. column
5. cell
6. labels, values, formulas
7. recalculation
8. "What if "
9. worksheet
10. range
11. Copy
12. Move
13. File
14. Print

Database Software: A Data Management Tool (2.8)

1. retrieve data, manipulate data, update data
2. file
3. record
4. field
5. database
6. database
7. data display
8. editing records
9. arithmetic

Graphics Software: A Data Presentation Tool (2.9)

1. pie chart
2. bar chart
3. line graph
4. analytical
5. data driven
6. command driven

Other Popular Microcomputer Applications (2.9)

1. data communications
2. desktop publishing

Integrated Software (2.10)

1. one
2. window

Guidelines for Purchasing Microcomputer Application Software (2.10)

1. task
2. computer
3. documented
4. purchase
5. value (price/product support)

Learning Aids and Support Tools for Application Users (2.10)

1. tutorial
2. online help
3. Trade books
4. Keyboard templates

Tips for Using Microcomputer Applications (2.11)

1. cursor
2. document
3. spelling
4. meaningful
5. templates
6. Save
7. assumptions
8. cells
9. labels
10. expansion
11. Highlight

12. Document
13. design
14. meaningful
15. ID
16. IDs
17. index
18. design
19. information
20. graphic
21. words
22. colors
23. consistent
24. projected

Review (2.12)

1. F
2. T
3. graphics
4. document preparation
5. T
6. grammar checker
7. manage numeric data
8. formulas
9. "what if "
10. multiple
11. record
12. Analytical
13. Data communication
14. windows
15. documentation
16. Online help

Chapter 3: Processing Data
Into Information

Overview of the Information Processing Cycle (3.2)

1. input
2. process
3. output
4. storage
5. keyboard

6. printer, computer screen
7. fixed disk, floppy disk
8. programs, data
9. Main memory
10. information

What Is Data and How Is It Organized? (3.3)

1. alphabetic, special, numeric
2. alphabetic, numeric, alphanumeric
3. field, record, file
4. any single data item could be circled
5. any row could be checked

6.   (4)

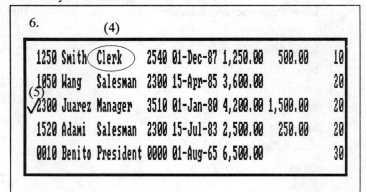

7. key field
8. database

Data Management (3.4)

1. techniques, methods, procedures, security, maintenance
2. data sources
3. available, accurate, reliable, timely
4. authorized access, backup
5. updating, adding, changing, deleting
6. data accuracy, data reliability, data timeliness

How the Information Processing Cycle Works (3.5)

1. main memory
2. computer program
3. processing
4. arithmetic operations
5. output
6. record

7. repeated
8. path
9. data
10. information
11. information
12. auxiliary storage

Methods of Processing Data Into Information (3.6)
1. interactive
2. batch
3. transaction
4. periodic, large
5. payroll, monthly bills

Qualities of Information (3.6)
1. meaningful, useful, cost effective

Review (3.7)
1. input
2. storage
3. software
4. programs
5. T
6. auxiliary
7. characters
8. field
9. alphanumeric
10. record
11. file
12. key
13. random
14. database
15. correct
16. integrity
17. F
18. maintenance
19. manipulated
20. arithmetic
21. repeat
22. compare
23. Reports

24. Storage
25. Interactive
26. batch
27. transaction
28. information

Chapter 4: Input to the Computer

What Is Input? (4.2)
1. programs, commands, user responses, data
2. main memory
3. keyboard, auxiliary storage
4. command
5. keyboard
6. user responses
7. main memory

The Keyboard (4.2)
1. terminal, personal computer
2. Number keys
3. Special characters
4. numeric keypad
5. Cursor control keys, arrow keys
6. insert key, delete key
7. function keys

Terminals (4.3)
1. dumb, intelligent, special purpose
2. independent
3. processing, programmable
4. uploading
5. point of sale

Other Input Devices (4.4)
1. mouse
2. ease of use
3. space, speed
4. touch screens
5. natural, speed
6. resolution, arm fatigue
7. light pen
8. digitizer
9. graphics tablet
10. Voice
11. no keying is necessary

Input Devices Designed for Specific Purposes (4.5)

1. optical character readers, optical mark readers, laser scanners, page scanners, image processing
2. reduced errors, data available immediately

User Interfaces (4.5)

1. hardware, software, communicate
2. respond to
3. control
4. information

Evolution of User Interface Software (4.6)

1. programmers, operators
2. difficult
3. prompts
4. alternatives
5. Menus
6. menu title
7. menu selection
8. menu prompt
9. sequential number
10. alphabetic
11. cursor positioning
12. reverse video
13. icon
14. users do not have to remember special commands, minimum of user training, user guided through the application
15. slow and restrictive to experienced users

Features of a User Interface (4.8)

1. response time, uncluttered, simple, user told how to recover, password

Data Entry for Interactive and Batch Processing (4.8)

1. output
2. online data entry
3. online, offline

An Example of Online Data Entry (4.8)

1. title and prompt
2. field to be entered
3. protected fields

Ergonomics (4.9)

1. plus or minus 7 degrees, antiglare, 10 to 20 degrees, 20 to 26 inches, 80 to 120 degrees

Review (4.9)

1. main memory
2. user
3. computer program
4. cursor
5. arrow keys
6. Function keys
7. T
8. programmable
9. point of sale
10. F
11. resolution
12. graphic
13. digital
14. banking
15. printed
16. optical character reader
17. test scoring
18. grocery stores
19. page scanners
20. image processing systems
21. Data collection
22. user interface
23. software
24. prompts
25. Menus
26. menu selection alternatives
27. graphic image
28. System responses
29. Response time
30. password
31. T
32. reverse video

33. distributed data entry
34. screen height
35. Transaction volume
36. transcription

Chapter 5: The Processor Unit

What Is the Processor Unit? (5.2)

1. memory
2. central processing unit
3. central processing unit
4. control unit, arithmetic/logic unit
5. fetch instruction
6. decode instruction
7. execute instruction
8. add/subtract
9. multiply/divide
10. compare
11. code
12. working
13. I/O
14. address
15. byte
16. 1024
17. 640
18. megabyte, gigabyte

How Programs and Data Are Represented in Memory (5.3)

1. numeric, special
2. byte
3. J O H N   D O E
4. $ 1 2 3 . 6 9
5. 8
6. bits
7. on, off
8. binary
9. ASCII
10. characters
11. 2

Parity (5.4)

1. right
2. Odd
3. Even
4. error
5. odd
6. transmission

Number Systems (5.5)

1. 10
2. 2
3. 16
4.

NUMBER SYSTEM	BASE	SYMBOLS USED
DECIMAL	10	0, 1, 2, 3, 4, 5, 6, 7, 8, 9
BINARY	2	0, 1
HEXADECIMAL	16	0, 1, 2, 3, 4, 5, 6, 7, 8, 9 A, B, C, D, E, F

5. zero
6. third
7. symbols
8. base
9. positional
10. zero
11. 2^2, or 4
12. 22
13. first
14. 76395
15. 4
16. 0101, 1010, C, B
17. AC

How the Processor Unit Executes Programs and Manipulates Data (5.7)

1. Machine language
2. operation code
3. value length
4. value 2 address
5. fetch, decode, execute, store

6. instruction

7. execution

Processor Speeds (5.8)

1. megahertz

2. MIPS

3. bus

4. width

5.

Busses:	TRANSFER SIZE (IN BITS)		
BUS WIDTH	8	16	32
8	1	2	4
16	1	1	2
32	1	1	1
	NUMBER OF TRANSFERS		

6. one

7. two

8. four

9. 640

10. one

11. sixteen

Architecture of Processor Units (5.9)

1. multiple

2. numeric, graphics

3. parallel

4. RISC

Types of Memory (5.9)

1. Vacuum tubes

2. core, semiconductor

3. RAM

4. ROM

Review (5.9)

1. control

2. main memory

3. 16,000

4. ten

5. 01011001

6. ASCII

7. 1

8. base

9. 2^2

10. 4

11. operation code

12. machine cycle

13. MIPS

14. 4

15. word size

16. coprocessor

17. semiconductor

18. volatile

Chapter 6: Output From the Computer

What Is Output? (6.2)

1. information

Common Types of Output (6.2)

1. hard copy

2. soft copy

3. Reports

4. Internal reports

5. External reports

6. detail report

7. summary report

8. exception report

9. Graphics

10. pie chart

11. bar chart

12. line chart

Printers (6.3)

1. front, hammer

2. Nonimpact

3. low speed

4. medium speed

5. high speed

6. very high speed

7. 80

8. 132

9. tractor, friction

10. bidirectional

Printers for Small and Medium Computers (6.4)

1. dot matrix
2. paper
3. ribbon
4. printing head
5. seven
6. standard
7. bold
8. graphics
9. daisy wheel
10. thermal
11. ink jet
12. laser

Printers for Large Computers (6.5)

1. chain
2. drive gear
3. ribbon
4. hammers
5. paper
6. ribbon
7. scalloped steel print band
8. hammer
9. magnet
10. paper
11. ink jet

Screens (6.6)

1. monitor, CRT, VDT
2. 80
3. cursor
4. arrow, rectangle, underline
5. scroll
6. blinking
7. color
8. LCD
9. pixels
10. Higher resolution
11. Color

Other Output Devices (6.7)

1. plotter
2. pen plotters, flatbed plotters, drum plotters, or electrostatic plotters
3. Computer output microfilm
4. Voice output
5. voice synthesizer

Review (6.7)

1. Output
2. reports and graphics
3. external
4. detail
5. graphics
6. pie chart
7. bar chart
8. impact or nonimpact
9. lines
10. all of the above
11. 8 1/2
12. tractor feed and friction feed
13. Dot matrix
14. daisy wheel
15. heat
16. laser
17. Band
18. page
19. scrolling
20. LCD -- liquid crystal display
21. plotter
22. T

Chapter 7: Auxiliary Storage

What Is Auxiliary Storage? (7.2)

1. nonvolatile
2. tape drive, disk drive
3. input/output
4. kilobytes, megabytes, gigabytes

Auxiliary Storage for Personal Computers (7.2)

1. convenient, reliable, low cost
2. 3 1/2, 5 1/4

3. mylar, plastic
4. metal oxide coating
5. disk jacket
6. hub, liner, or recording window
7. plastic
8. tracks, sectors
9. track
10. sector
11.

DISKETTE TYPE	TRACKS PER DISK	SECTORS PER TRACK	TRACK NUMBERING
5 1/4"	40	9	0-39
3 1/2"	80	9	0-39

12. timing, sector
13. index, sector
14. recording density, number of tracks, number of sides
15. 2
16. bits
17. seek time, latency, settling time, transfer rate
18. Don't touch the disk surface.
    Don't bend the disk.
    Don't expose the disk to excessive sunlight.
    Don't expose the disk to magnetic fields.
    Don't use an eraser on the disk label.
    Don't place a heavy object on the disk.
19. Use felt-tip marker on labels.
    Store disks in their dust jackets.
20. platters
21. larger, faster
22. mounted, sealed
23. hard card
24. spindle
25. platters
26. access arms (actuators)
27. read/write heads
28. millionth
29. head crash

30. 10, 100
31. 25, 80
32. online storage, large capacity, faster access
33. fast access, high capacity, portable, easily secured
34.

35. uncovered, covered
36. backup

Auxiliary Storage for Medium and Large Computers (7.6)

1. DASD
2. fixed, removable
3. disk pack
4. stand-alone cabinet
5. 10, 300
6. sector method, cylinder method
7. backup, data transfer
8. 300; 3,600
9. 100
10. supply reel
11. take-up reel
12. read/write head
13. vacuum columns
14. EBCDIC, 9
15. 800; 6,250
16. 38,000
17. interblock
18. logical
19. physical

Other Forms of Auxiliary Storage (7.8)

1. billion
2. CDROM, WORM
3. solid-state, mass

Review (7.8)

1. secondary storage
2. F
3. 3 1/2, 5 1/4
4. defining the tracks and sectors on the diskette surface
5. T
6. the number of sectors on the disk
7. bits recorded per inch
8. latency
9. to position the read/write head over the proper track
10. F
11. F
12. storage features of a hard disk
13. backing up data onto a cartridge tape
14. hard card
15. cylinder
16. T
17. cartridge tape
18. logical records, physical records
19. the grouping of logical records
20. inability to be reused
21. T
22. F

Chapter 8: File Organization and Databases

What Is a File? (8.2)

1. file
2. fields
3. field

Types of File Organization (8.2)

1. sequential, indexed, direct or relative
2. printing, backup
3. 55
4. key field, disk address
5. random
6. relative
7. hashing

8.

FILE TYPE	TYPE OF STORAGE	ACCESS METHOD
SEQUENTIAL	Tape or Disk	Sequential
INDEXED	Disk	Sequential * or Random
DIRECT (RELATIVE)	Disk	Sequential * or Random

How Is Data in Files Maintained? (8.3)

1. adding, changing, deleting

Databases: A Better Way to Manage Data and Information (8.4)

1. multiple separate files
2. database

What Is a Database? (8.4)

1.

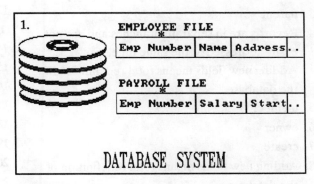

DATABASE SYSTEM

1. continued

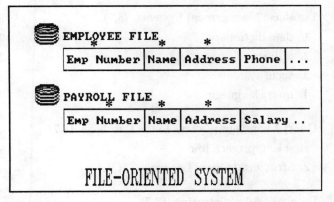

FILE-ORIENTED SYSTEM

2. database management system
3. file management system

Why Use a Database? (8.5)
1. improved data integrity, reduced data redundancy, integrated files, improved data security

Types of Database Organization (8.5)
1. network, relational, hierarchical
2. file
3. record
4. field
5. domain
6. link
7. Data relationship doesn't have to be predefined. Adding new fields only requires defining the fields in the appropriate table.
8. parent
9. parent-child
10. parent
11. child
12. child
13. parent
14. Records are in separate branches and are not easily addressed at the same time.
    Adding new fields means total redefinition of the database.
15. member
16. owner
17. create
18. Adding new fields means total redefinition of the database.

Database Management Systems (8.7)
1. data dictionary
2. utilities
3. security
4. query language

Query Languages: Access to the Database (8.7)
1. select, project, join
2. Structured Query Language (SQL)

Database Administration (8.7)
1. database administrator

Managing Data on a Personal Computer (8.7)
1. mainframe

Summary of Databases (8.8)
1. organizing
2. redundant
3. Query

Review (8.8)
1. records
2. T
3. record
4. auxiliary storage
5. sequential
6. access speed is slow
7. sequence
8. disk
9. T
10. position
11. hashing
12. collision
.13. updating
14. T
15. multiple
16. Database management
17. File management
18. reduced data integrity
19. relational
20. link
21. flexibility
22. hierarchical
23. root
24. fast
25. multiple
26. T
27. English-like
28. rows
29. fields
30. relational
31. database administrator
32. F
33. dBASE
34. multiple

Chapter 9: Data Communications

What Is Data Communications? (9.2)
1. transmission of data
2. communication channel
3. communication equipment
4. computer or terminal

Communication Channels (9.2)
1. twisted pair wire
2. coaxial cable
3. fiber optics
4. microwave
5. uplink
6. downlink
7. earth stations

Line Configurations (9.3)
1. point-to-point
2. multidrop

Characteristics of Communication Channels (9.4)
1. digital, analog
2. synchronous
3. asynchronous
4. simplex
5. half-duplex
6. full-duplex
7. bits per second

Communication Equipment (9.4)
1. modem
2. internal
3. acoustic coupler
4. multiplexor
5. Polling

Communication Software (9.6)
1. dialing, terminal emulation, data encryption

Communication Networks (9.6)
1. information resource sharing, hardware resource sharing, or network control unit

2. wide area network

Network Configurations (9.6)
1. star network
2. bus network
3. ring network

The Personal Computer and Data Communications (9.7)
1. home banking, electronic shopping, commercial databases, electronic bulletin boards

Review (9.7)
1. data communications
2. communication channel
3. communication equipment
4. personal computer or terminal
5. T
6. one signal at a time
7. multiple signals
8. satellite
9. Line configurations
10. T
11. a host computer
12. Digital
13. Analog
14. synchronous
15. asynchronous
16. T
17. modem
18. circuit board inside the computer
19. an acoustic coupler
20. multiplexing
21. network
22. star
23. all of the above

Chapter 10: Operating Systems and System Software

What Is System Software? (10.2)
1. system, application
2. System
3. starts up the computer, stores and retrieves files, loads and executes application programs, performs utility functions

4. Application
5. spreadsheet, database, graphics, word processing

What Is an Operating System? (10.2)
1. equipment
2. monitor, kernel, executive, master program, control program
3. memory

Loading an Operating System (10.3)
1. operating system
2. computer
3. operating system
4. application
5. execution
6. commands

Types of Operating Systems (10.3)
1. simultaneous
2. programs
3. single program
4. multiprogramming or multitasking
5. multiprocessing
6. virtual machine
7. more than one
8. one or more than one (multiuser)
9. more than one on each CPU
10. more than one on each CPU
11. more than one on each operating system
12. more than one on each operating system

Functions of Operating Systems (10.5)
1. allocating system resources
2. monitoring activities
3. utilities
4. time slicing
5. time slicing without priority
6. time slicing with priority
7. partitioning
8. active
9. segmentation

10. paging
11. swapping
12. multiple
13. spooling
14. CPU utilization, response time
15. security
16. utilities

Popular Operating Systems   (10.7)
1. proprietary operating systems
2. UNIX
3. OS/2
4. portable operating systems
5. MS-DOS

Review (10.7)
1. F
2. systems
3. T
4. T
5. ROM
6. T
7. multiprocessing
8. T
9. F
10. Time
11. Paging
12. F
13. T
14. T
15. utilities
16. F

Chapter 11: Commercial Application Software

What Is Commercial Application Software? (11.2)
1. has been previously written and is available for purchase
2. general, specific

General Application Software (11.2)

1. productivity tools
2. word processing, spreadsheets, database, graphics
3. desktop publishing, electronic mail, project management
4. Desktop publishing
5. What You See Is What You Get
6. communication channels
7. planning, scheduling, task analysis, resources, costs and budgets

Functional Application Software (11.3)

1. task, function
2. horizontal applications
3. vertical applications

The Decision to Make or Buy Application Software (11.3)

1. custom
2. commercial
3. custom software

How to Acquire Commercial Application Software (11.3)

1. evaluate the application requirements, identify potential software vendors, evaluate the software alternatives, purchase the software, install the software
2. identify key features of the application, determine your current transaction volumes and estimate their growth over the next one to three years, decide if the software needs to work with any existing software or equipment, issue a request for proposal (RFP) to prospective vendors who may have a possible software solution, identify potential software vendors
3. software houses
4. system houses
5. trade publications
6. computer magazines
7. consultants

8. demonstrations, user references, testing
9. software license
10. installing the software
11. train the users, test the system, have a users manual available

Review (11.5)

1. commercial application software
2. functional
3. tasks that are commonly performed in all types of businesses
4. T
5. Desktop publishing
6. T
7. T
8. project management
9. specific tasks or functions
10. horizontal
11. Vertical
12. custom software
13. a vertical application
14. requirements
15. T
16. T
17. performance
18. software license

Chapter 12: The Information System Development Life Cycle

What Is an Information System? (12.2)

1. collection of elements
2. equipment, software, data, personnel, users, procedures

Types of Information Systems (12.2)

1. operational systems, management information systems, decision support systems, expert systems

What Is the Information System Development Life Cycle? (12.2)

1. Phase 1--analysis
   Phase 2--design
   Phase 3--development
   Phase 4--implementation
   Phase 5--maintenance
2. Project management, documentation

Phase 1--Analysis (12.3)

1. the separation of a system into its parts to determine how the system works
2. problem definition
3. system analysis
4. interviews, questionnaires, reviewing current system documentation
5. the output of the current system, the procedures used to produce the output, the input to the current system
6. design tools
7. feasibility study
8. cost/benefit analysis

Phase 2--Design (12.4)

1. logical
2. physical
3. Top-down design
4. Bottom-up design
5. output design
6. dialogue
7. database design
8. input data, output information
9. standard flowchart
10. controls
11. source document controls, input controls, processing controls, accounting controls
12. F
13. design review
14. prototyping

Phase 3--Development (12.6)

1. program development, equipment acquisition

Phase 4--Implementation (12.6)

1. training and education, conversion, postimplementation evaluation

Phase 5--Maintenance (12.6)

1. the process of supporting the system after it is implemented
2. performance monitoring, change management, error correction

Review (12.6)

1. information system
2. software
3. operational system
4. decision support system
5. management information system
6. expert system
7. T
8. Project management
9. Documentation
10. analysis phase
11. detailed system analysis
12. F
13. design phase
14. all of the above
15. T
16. system flowchart
17. prototype
18. development phase
19. F
20. implementation phase
21. training and education
22. T
23. maintenance phase
24. T

Chapter 13: Program Development

What Is a Computer Program? (13.2)

1. instructions, data, process, information

What Is Program Development? (13.2)

1. review specs
2. design
3. code
4. test
5. finalize documentation

Step 1--Review of Program Specifications (13.2)

1. data flow diagrams, system flowcharts, process specifications, data dictionary, screen formats, report layouts
2. analyst, users
3. programmer

Step 2--Program Design (13.3)

1. logical solution
2. Structured program design
3. modules, control structures, single entry/single exit
4. subroutines
5. Structure or hierarchy charts
6. hierarchy charts, modules
7. sequence, selection, iteration
8. sequence
9. Selection or if-then-else structure
10. Iteration or looping
11. do-while
12. do-until
13. Single entry/single exit
14. flowcharts, pseudocode, Warnier-Orr
15. decision
16. terminal
17. input/output
18. predefined process
19. processing
20. offpage connector
21. connector
22. preparation
23. Pseudocode, eliminates drawing symbols
24. output
25. structured walkthrough
26. Systems analysts
27. review logic for errors, improve program design

Step 3--Program Coding (13.5)

1. Program coding

Step 4--Program Testing (13.5)

1. desk checking, syntax error checking, logic testing, debugging
2. similar to proofreading a letter
3. identifying violations of the program language's grammar rules
4. using test data (expected and unexpected data) to test the program
5. locating and correcting program errors during testing

Step 5--Finalizing Program Documentation (13.5)

1. narrative description, program flowcharts, pseudocode, program listings, test results, comments within program

Program Maintenance (13.6)

1. errors

What Is a Programming Language? (13.6)

1. communicate

Categories of Programming Languages (13.6)

1. machine language, assembly language, high-level languages, fourth-generation languages
2. Machine language
3. converted
4. mnemonics
5. symbolic addressing
6. Macroinstructions
7. contain program statements, are usually machine independent, are converted to machine language by a compiler or an interpreter
8. source program
9. error listing
10. source program statement
11. interpreter
12. machine language instructions

13. very high-level languages, nonprocedural
14. what, how
15. database query language
16. natural

Programming Languages Used Today (13.8)

1. Beginner's All-purpose Symbolic Instruction Code
2. microcomputers, minicomputers
3. COmmon Business Oriented Language
4. business
5. systems
6. FORmula TRANslator
7. mathematical equations
8. Blaise Pascal
9. structured
10. Augusta Ada Byron
11. programs
12. Report Program Generator
13. reports
14. It uses special forms filled out describing the report.
15. ALGOL
16. APL
17. FORTH
18. LISP, PROLOG
19. LOGO
20. MODULA-2
21. PILOT
22. PL/1

Application Generators (13.10)

1. program generators
2. source programs
3. menu generator
4. screen generator

How to Choose a Programming Language (13.10)

1. programming standards, portability, language suitability, maintenance require-ments, programmer expertise, language availability, interfacing needs

Review (13.11)

1. all of the above
2. review of program specifications
3. modules
4. iteration
5. UNTIL
6. a single entry/exit
7. testing the program
8. all of the above
9. an ongoing process
10. programmer
11. T
12. F
13. translate
14. what verses how
15. Pascal
16. COBOL and RPG
17. generators
18. T

Chapter 14: Career Opportunities in the Age of Information Processing

The Information Processing Industry (14.2)

1. the computer equipment industry, the computer software industry, information processing professionals

What Are the Career Opportunities in Information Processing? (14.2)

1. operations, data administration, system analysis and design, programming, information center
2. Operations
3. database administration, quality assurance
4. systems analysis, forms design and control
5. system
6. consulting, training
7. Sales
8. consultant
9. T

Compensation and Growth Trends for Information Processing Careers (14.3)

1. communications
2. $24,300
   $30,000
   $22,000
   $23,200
   $28,600
   $27,600

Preparing for a Career in Information Processing (14.3)

1. computer engineering, computer information systems, computer science
2. computer design engineer, service and repair technician
3. information processing manager, database administrator, systems analyst, business applications programmer, computer operator, data entry operator
4. computer scientist, language design specialist, systems software specialist
5. user groups

Career Development in the Information Processing Industry (14.4)

1. professional
2. Certification

Review (14.4)

1. computers
2. computer equipment
3. IBM
4. all of the above
5. programmer
6. T
7. teaching and consulting
8. Sales representatives
9. T
10. Consultants
11. demand
12. all of the above

13. business
14. Computer science
15. Computer engineering
16. T
17. Professional organizations
18. T
19. T

Chapter 15: Trends and Issues in the Information Age

Information Systems in Business (15.2)

1. word processing
2. electronic mail
3. voice mail
4. desktop publishing
5. facsimile
6. image processing
7. teleconferencing or video conferencing
8. computer-aided design
9. Computer-aided engineering (CAE)
10. factory
11. product design
12. production planning
13. manufacturing
14. product distribution

Bringing the Information Age Home (15.3)

1. personal
2. personal services, control of home systems, telecommuting, education, entertainment
3. Computer-aided instruction (CAI)
4. Step 1: Become computer literate.
   Step 2: Define and prioritize the tasks you want to perform on your computer.
   Step 3: Select software packages that best meet your needs.
   Step 4: Select equipment that will run software you have selected.
   Step 5: Select the suppliers for software and equipment.
   Step 6: Purchase software and equipment.

Social Issues (15.5)

1. software theft or software piracy, unauthorized access and use, malicious damage, viruses

Review (15.5)

1. productivity
2. word processing
3. Electronic mail
4. T
5. CAD
6. CAM
7. CAE
8. T
9. T
10. T
11. telecommuting
12. education
13. F
14. T
15. security
16. T

Introduction To DOS

Introduction (DOS 2)

1. operating system
2. disk operating system
3. PC-DOS
4. MS-DOS
5. versions

Using the Disk Operating System (DOS 2)

1. DOS
2. booting
3. hard
4. Ctrl Alt Del
5. date, time
6. prompt
7. default
8. B:
9. enter
10. C

Entering Disk Operating System (DOS) Commands (DOS 3)

1. COPY, DIR, ERASE, RENAME, DEL, CLS
2. External

Directory Command (DIR) (DOS 3)

1. DIR
2. DIR   B:
3. Ctrl Break
4. DIR   /P
5. DIR   /W

Formatting a Diskette (DOS 4)

1. FORMAT   b:
2. FORMAT   /S
3. FORMAT   /V

CLS Command (DOS 4)

1. clear screen

Managing Data and Program Files on Disks (DOS 4)

1. data
2. program
3. disk
4. path
5. filename
6. extension
7. com, exe
8. Batch

Copy Command (DOS 5)

1. COPY   DOSQUIZ.DOC   B:
2. backup
3. source
4. target
5. global
6. asterisk(*)
7. COPY   *.*   B:
8. COPY   *.COM   B:
9. COPY   A:G*.*   B:
10. wildcard
11. COPY   *.BA?   B:
12. A:>COPY   C:\BATCH*.*   B:

13. A:>DIR B:*.EXE
14. C:\WORK>COPY *.* \BACKUP
15. C:>DIR \WP\FILES*.DOC
16. C:\UTILITY>COPY *.EXE A:
17. C:\BASIC>COPY *.BAS A:
18. A:>COPY *.BAT C:\BATCH

RENAME Command (DOS 7)
1. name
2. RENAME NOTECOPY DOSFILE
3. RENAME *.BAK *.BAC

ERASE and DEL Commands (DOS 8)
1. remove

Using Directories and Subdirectories (DOS 8)
1. root
2.

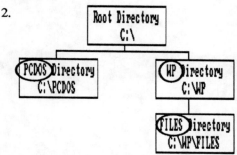

3. Make Directory (MD)
4. Change Directory (CD)
5. default
6. files
7. Remove Directory (RD)

Loading a Program (DOS 9)
1. filename

Review   (DOS 9)
1. booting
2. T
3. Alt
4. a or c, depending on the default drive
5. T
6. T
7. c or d

8. FORMAT
9. FORMAT B:/V
10. F
11. DRIVE\PATH\FILENAME.EXTENSION
12. T
13. backup copies
14. all of the above
15. source
16. target
17. RENAME TEST1.DOC QUIZ2.DOC
18. either a or c
19. root
20. directories and subdirectories
21. make a directory on a disk
22. CD \123\DATA
23. T
24. remove a directory